Body Language

Body Language

Human and divine imagery in the Bible

John Cox

kevin mayhew

www.kevinmayhew.com

kevin mayhew

First published in Great Britain in 2015 by Kevin Mayhew Ltd
Buxhall, Stowmarket, Suffolk IP14 3BW
Tel: +44 (0) 1449 737978 Fax: +44 (0) 1449 737834
E-mail: info@kevinmayhew.com

www.kevinmayhew.com

9 8 7 6 5 4 3 2 1 0

ISBN 978 1 84867 776 0
Catalogue No. 1501474

Cover design by Justin Minns
© Images used under licence from Shutterstock Inc.
Edited by Nicki Copeland

Printed and bound in Great Britain

Contents

About the author

Having spent rather a long time at various universities including Cambridge, Oxford and the University College of Rhodesia and Nyasaland, John was ordained to a curacy in the diocese of Liverpool in 1968. He spent a second curacy in an inner-city ex-slum parish in Birmingham and became rector in the same parish. After a five-year period at Church House, Westminster where he was Senior Selection Secretary, helping to select ordinands, he was made Canon Treasurer at Southwark Cathedral and Diocesan Director of Ordinands and Post-ordination training.

Following four years as Vicar of Roehampton he moved to become Archdeacon of Sudbury in the Diocese of St Edmundsbury and Ipswich in 1995. When he retired in 2006 he was asked to be the part-time Diocesan Director of Education, a job he did for nearly four and a half years before retiring for a second time. It has been during these retirement years that John has been writing for Kevin Mayhew, in between being chair of governors at a primary academy, playing golf and enjoying river cruises.

Introduction

We are obsessed with our bodies. At least, that appears to be true of the West in recent years and is arguably true of peoples throughout the ages and in differing cultures. We seek to adorn our bodies, to modify them, to deny them, to abuse them, to nurture them, to protect them, to preserve them.

This is not surprising. We are bodily creatures. We may be more than just our physical bodies but we can't deny our bodily existence. It is through our bodies that we communicate and are recognised. They shape and give expression to our identity. They enable or impede our mobility, our activities, our sense of worth, our social interaction. What our words sometimes fail to communicate, our bodies can convey. What we wish to hide from being spoken out can be betrayed by our bodies. They 'spill the beans'. Our bodies have a language of their own and, to a lesser or greater extent, we all have a skill in reading body language. We also draw upon the body for countless metaphors and as a source of imagery for what is intangible and spiritual, including for our descriptions of God.

In the early fifteenth century, two Flemish brothers, Hubert and Jan van Eyck, produced one of the great masterpieces of Western art: the Ghent altar piece known as The Adoration of the Lamb. (The best website to view this altar piece is http://closertovaneyck.kikirpa.be). Although of outstanding artistic and religious significance, it is surrounded by controversy and speculation, not only from art historians but from theologians as well. It is currently the subject of a five-year programme of restoration and research.

In total, the altar piece is constructed from 12 separate panels. The main panel depicts the Lamb of God on an altar set in an expansive landscape surrounded by figures in various groups, such as Just Judges, Knights of Christ, holy pilgrims and holy hermits, and saints of both the Old and New Testaments. Above this lower central panel there is a depiction of God, with Mary to the left and John the Baptist to the right. They are bracketed by the figures of Adam and Eve.

It is the figure of God and the figures of Adam and Eve that are of particular interest for this short study on the body in Scripture, and as reflected on in theology and Christian spirituality.

Few question the interpretation of the richly robed figure holding a sceptre and wearing a three-tiered crown. It is God. But is it God the Father or God the Son? The kingly figure with the three-tiered crown seated on a throne bearing the inscription, 'This is the Almighty God through His Divine Majesty', and wearing a golden stole with the embroidered text from the Mass '(Dominus Deus) Sabaot – Lord of Hosts', is thought by some scholars to be the figure of God the Father. This is supported by the fact that the figure does not bear the nail marks of the crucifixion in his hands, that he has shoes on his feet and carries a sceptre rather than a book, which would be more usual if it were God the Son.

Against this there are indications that the figure is actually of the Christ. The figure sits between Mary and John the Baptist, an arrangement traditionally known as Deesis (supplication). Without exception, in all other Christian art and iconography the central figure is of Jesus. There are also motifs in the tapestry on the back of the throne which are associated with Christ – the pelican feeding its young from its own blood, and the vine leaves which are a further reference to the Communion wine, the blood of Christ (see 'I am the true vine' in John 15:1). The name 'Jesus Christ' appears above the pelican. John is pointing with his index finger to the figure, which would indicate that the figure is the Son: in John's Gospel the Baptist 'points out' the presence of Jesus as the Messiah, the Lamb, the Son of God (John 1:29).

The enthroned figure could be either God the Father or the ascended Christ. The debate continues. But it could be argued that a choice is not necessary. The artists may have intended an ambiguity that is spiritually sophisticated and implies the mystery of God. The figure is God both as Father and Son. At the top of the panel immediately beneath the figure of God there is a dove, symbol of the Holy Spirit. The figure's three-tiered crown underlines the theological point that God is in fact Trinity. Was all this the artists' original intention and meaning? It is impossible to know.

The question for an artist is how do you, in fact, attempt to depict God? To do so through a human bodily form might appear obvious, but this runs into further questions and a potential theological ambiguity. God is a spiritual, not a physical being, and is not just a human being writ large or especially splendid.

The Jews were fiercely antagonistic towards any attempt to make depictions of God – even his name was too holy to be written or pronounced in full. The Old Testament is full of prophetic denunciation for those who made or worshipped idols. Ways were found to describe God's interaction with people and events that avoided conveying a sense of his actual physical presence – for example, where an angel or messengers take the place of God. In the report of Moses' most famous encounter with God, there is simply the burning bush to attract his attention and a voice that addresses Moses. Some accounts in Exodus say that Moses spoke with God 'face to face' (33:11), but elsewhere we are told that all Moses saw of God was where he had been. For his own safety, Moses was not allowed to see God (Exodus 33:17-23). The account of the

Garden of Eden tells of God walking there in the cool of the evening and hunting out Adam and Eve who were hiding out of fear and guilt (Genesis 3:8). But such intimate and physical descriptions are reserved for a world at or prior to the Fall.

Accounts of God in any physical sense are making use of imagery and are not attempts to provide direct descriptions of his nature or action. He may be described as speaking, but there is no suggestion he has an actual mouth and voice box. The account of his moulding of Adam like a sculptor modelling clay is a poetic device to convey God's direct involvement in creating, not because the author believed God has hands. God is not physical, not a 'superman'.

But this assertion, which seems so clear from a reasonable interpretation of the Old Testament accounts, becomes more problematic when we enter the New Testament world. For here, a central act of faith is the declaration that the unseen, eternal, transcendent God has, in Jesus, taken human shape. In St John's words, 'The Word became flesh and lived among us' (John 1:14). God as man, with a physical human form. For the Christian, this is not on a par with Greek myths, where the gods came to earth in various shapes, including human, to act out their passions and jealousies. For the Christian, this is a statement about God's direct and actual involvement in the physical world as a physical being. There may well be complexities to the notion of 'incarnation', but they are not solved by seeking to make Jesus less than fully human, fully physical.

Because of Jesus, there is a 'legitimate' way of picturing God in physical form, and this subtly changes the overall way we understand God. But it is not simply that we can now think of God as in some sense physical the 'super man' the Jews rightly refused to countenance. We cannot and must not. There is a relationship between the physical, human aspect of Jesus and the eternal, spiritual nature of Christ who is the Son of God. The Christological conundrum, 'fully human and fully divine', is brought together in the name of Jesus properly understood: not Jesus Christ but Jesus the Christ, or Jesus who is the Christ, the Son of God – Emmanuel, God with us. So while an artist may legitimately depict Jesus as fully and physically human, this will never be the whole story, and especially not so when attempts are made to depict the ascended Christ, the Christ in glory. Hence some of the reasons for the debate about the Van Eyck figure.

Incarnation not only presents us with a radical way of understanding God and his relationship to the physical world; it also presents us with a radical new way of understanding the place of human beings, including their physical nature. Christianity has tended to have an ambivalent attitude towards the body. On the one hand it is intrinsically related to our individual and corporate identity. It is therefore precious, and the loss of any significant part of our body – our features, a limb, a breast – can arouse a deep sense of grieving and a change in our self-perception. Theologically, our bodies are part of God's gift to us and are seen as the abode of God's Spirit within us. St Paul therefore called them temples (1 Corinthians 6:19). But they are also what give rise to and express our passions, and are therefore seen as dangerous. The pleasures of the bodily senses can all too easily give rise to lusts and greeds, especially those associated with sex. The body has therefore also been seen as something requiring discipline and control, to the point where its denial has been a focus of much ascetic and puritanical spirituality.

In the Van Eyck altar piece, Adam and Eve are depicted, for the first time in Western art, in a realistic and individualised way. They are not idealised figures, nor are they humiliated or torn by guilt. There is almost a calm serenity about them. They are naked and not ashamed. Although they modestly cover their nakedness, the artist still depicts their pubic hair. It was only in a much later nineteenth-century version that they were given furs to cover their bodies! It is, of course, a matter of opinion as to whether this reveals a healthier attitude towards sex and the body.

This book looks at the way the Bible uses language about the body as a symbolic description of God and the Church to convey spiritual and theological truths. It also looks at passages in the Scriptures where the body plays an important part, such as in the various healing miracles. At various points, questions will be raised for the reader to consider and reflect on.

Chapter one
God

If we could fully describe God, he would be less than God. It sounds like a quote, but if it is I don't know who said it. But it's a truth we almost instinctively feel. However hard we try to say what God is like, he remains a mystery. All our descriptions fall short. We try to move from what we know to what we do not, and although we may inch ahead little by little, there comes a point where God in all his fullness eludes us. Part of us wishes it weren't so. We want God whole, no mysteries, no remainders that we cannot grasp and understand. And part of us knows that what tantalisingly does elude us is important; it is right for the mystery to remain. Seeing in a glass darkly is all we can expect now, and all we can cope with. Later it may be different (1 Corinthians 13:12, KJV).

Objections might be raised that I am forgetting two important points for faith:

- What we cannot fathom out, God has revealed.
- In Jesus we see the fullness of God revealed.

I certainly do not wish to deny the reality of revelation: that God has made known what we could not have concluded from our own arguments, imaginings or deductions, including things about his own nature and purposes. But that is not the same as saying we know everything about God. And even if we go along with the writer of the letter to the Colossians that in Jesus 'the fullness of God was pleased to dwell' (Colossians 1:19), it would be a brave person who claims to know everything about Jesus, and we certainly have no knowledge of exactly what he looked like.

But, of course, all this does not mean we have no idea of what God is like – the Bible gives us plenty of clues, and in Jesus we see in human form the way God is. Just because we don't – and this side of heaven can't – know everything about God does not mean we can say nothing. It simply points us to a proper sense of humility and a recognition that our knowledge is partial.

The language we use will, at best, be a series of approximations. All our talk about God and all our descriptions tell us what he is like, rather than what he is in himself. He is like a father who loves us and holds us in his arms; he is like a king who rules in a kingdom of love and justice; it is as though he speaks to us and walks with us. These are among the best words we can use to express our experience of God and what he shows himself to be like. They speak adequately, truly, but we must never think they say everything. I know of no higher, truer, better way of describing God than saying he is love. But however much the meaning of that word 'love' is shaped by all I learn about God through the Bible, through Jesus, through prayer and through other people, the word remains a human construct and therefore limited. I have a profound hope and belief that if and when the time comes that I see God 'face to face', I shall experience something that is fuller and richer than I have ever imagined when using 'love' as a description of God. For the time being, I trust that it is pointing in the right direction.

- As you think about God or as you pray, do you attempt to picture God?
- Do you find it easier to imagine God or Jesus?
- Whichever you choose, why do you think this is so?

I have laboured the point because in this book there will be a lot of descriptions of and about God, drawing in particular on 'body language' – aspects of the human body applied to God. On the one hand this has the danger of making it sound as though we are merely making God in our own image. There are plenty of critics of the Christian faith who would say that is exactly what we do. On the other hand there is the danger of taking the descriptions too literally, as though God actually has hands and feet. We have to steer a path along the ridge between these two chasms and do our best not to fall in.

a. Face

The younger generation delight in modern forms of communication – hours on the mobile phone or finger chattering texting. Much of their communication with one another is via social media. There are fears that while it is good that they are contacting one another, they will nevertheless lose out on some of the more subtle social skills that are involved in face-to-face encounters. It is not without reason that our faces have evolved to include numerous muscles, giving the potential for a large range of different, varied and very subtle facial expressions. When survival may well have depended on it, it was important to be able to read correctly the signs of another person's intentions, to know whether they were friendly or hostile. It is not for nothing that lovers gaze into each other's eyes, or boxers square up to one another before a bout, their faces only inches apart. The Maori war dances and chants, the haka, include grotesque facial expressions as a way of putting fear into the opposition – as many a rugby team facing the All Blacks know. It is a matter of deep concern to Asians to 'lose face'.

We may be known by our DNA, our handwriting, the way we dress or our fingerprints, but the most usual form of recognition is through what we look like – our faces – although as an identical twin I am conscious that recognition cannot always be guaranteed. The importance we give to what we look like generally focuses on what our face looks like. Either in response to demand or as part of the creation of a demand, the beauty products industry is large and growing. In the three months from January to March 2012 beauty sales globally were up 14% at $2.25 billion.[1] In a time of recession in the US it was found that women would cut down on many purchases, but not on beauty products.[2] Of all spending on beauty products and personal care, 47% is on facial care and make-up.[3]

The loss of any part of our body evokes a grieving and a modification of our self-image. This is particularly true if the loss or radical change involves what we look like. Deformity of our face can be significantly embarrassing, perhaps more to others than even to ourselves. Simon Weston, the Falklands veteran who suffered horrendous injuries and burns to his face, is recognised for his bravery not only in surviving his injuries but in becoming a public figure in spite of them.

While what we look like does not determine our identity, the two are certainly significantly related. We feel we know someone better if we know what they look like – although it can sometimes come as a surprise actually to see someone whom we have only previously known by listening to their voice or reading their letters and emails. This has been true, for example, for regular listeners of the radio programme *The Archers*. Having established a clear image of the various characters in their minds, they find it difficult to relate them to the appearance of the actors who play the characters.

---

1. The Beauty Company Facts and Figures, June 2012. Available at
   www.thebeautycompany.com (accessed 15 January 2015).
2. Reuters – Patricia Reaney, New York, 5 July 2012.
3. The Beauty Company Facts and Figures June 2012.

Since 2010, when the first full facial transplant was carried out, it has been possible for a person who has 'lost' their face to receive that of another person. The medical issues involved are enormous, but so are the ethical and psychological concerns. Recipients require not only lengthy medical care after the operation, but also psychological counselling. Because what we look like is more than skin deep – it also depends on bone structure and muscle shape – the 'new' face is always a mix of what both the recipient and the donor looked like. It raises deep questions of who the person then feels themself to be.

> • How important to you is the way you look?
> • Does the physical appearance of other people affect the way you think about them and treat them?

What our faces mean to us lies behind how the face has been used in descriptions of God. When the writer of the book of Exodus wanted to convey the intimate relationship that Moses had with Yahweh, it spoke not only of his speaking with God or being instructed by God but also of their meeting together 'face to face'. Such a 'direct' meeting with God is specific to Moses, and even then the record is contradictory. In recording Moses' encounters with Yahweh at the Tent of Meeting the writer emphasises the closeness of the relationship: 'Thus the Lord used to speak to Moses face to face, as one speaks to a friend' (Exodus 33:11). But when it came to Moses' request to see the glory of the Lord, this was denied:

> And he said, 'I will make all my goodness pass before you, and will proclaim before you the name "The Lord"; and I will be gracious to whom I will be gracious, and

will show mercy on whom I will show mercy. But', he said, 'you cannot see my face; for no one shall see me and live.' And the Lord continued, 'See there is a place by me where you shall stand on the rock; and while my glory passes by I will put you in a cleft of the rock, and I will cover you with my hand until I have passed by; then I will take away my hand, and you shall see my back; but my face shall not be seen.'

Exodus 33:19-23

That the Lord should have gone so far as to declare his name was itself a sign of the special relationship Moses had with him, a person's name being a powerful aspect of their identity. But to see the Lord's face was not allowed. The refusal is understood as part of the Lord's care of Moses – he didn't want Moses to die. And the description of Moses only seeing God's back is true of most of our experience – we see where God has acted, where he has been. We are less certain of knowing where he will be or how he will act in the future.

This intimate relationship between Moses and the Lord was in many ways unique, and of course it reflected, or gave rise to, the special authority that Moses had within the tradition not only as the one who led the people out of Egypt and through the wilderness but also as the one through whom the Lord gave the people the Law.

In the account of Moses convening the people of Israel to remind them of their covenant with the Lord and the giving of his Laws at Horeb, Moses does say that the Lord spoke to the people 'face to face' out of the fire, although this is immediately qualified by the following comment: 'At that time I was standing between the Lord and you to declare to you the words of the Lord; for you were afraid because of the fire and did not go up the mountain' (Deuteronomy 5:4, 5). The writer is here making a contrast between the direct way in which the Lord met his people on this occasion and how he had been experienced by their ancestors. It says more about how he understood the Lord to have approached his people rather than what the people actually saw.

Only in the Garden of Eden, prior to the Fall, had there been a fuller, more immediate relationship. Adam and Eve are said to have talked and walked with God. He instructed them, he searched for them as they hid out of guilt and shame and he drove them from the garden. It is not made explicit that they saw God's face – we are free to assume they did.

To be allowed into the presence of a king was a privilege and a sign of his favour. The king would show his face to the courtier, the petitioner or the diplomat and would welcome them and speak with them. Refusal to allow someone to come into the king's presence was a sign of his disfavour. He would 'hide his face' from that person. In describing this sign of a king's favour, older translations of the Bible, such as the Authorised Version, refer specifically to the face. A modern translation, on the other hand, such as the NRSV, indicates the same sense of favour by saying that the king turned to the people. The meaning is the same: to show favour, a king faces his people, as when Solomon blessed the people at the dedication of the Temple: 'Then the king turned round and blessed all the assembly of Israel' (2 Chronicles 6:3 NRSV); 'And the king turned his face, and blessed the whole congregation of Israel' (2 Chronicles 6:3 Authorised Version).

The same imagery was used in descriptions of God in indicating his attitude to his people or to the nations. If God declared that he would turn or had turned his face from the people, it revealed his displeasure with them. As far as an enemy nation was concerned, it was a sign of hostility. In his final address to Moses, the Lord predicted how the people would turn to other gods, breaking the covenant made with the Lord, and spoke of his response:

> My anger will be kindled against them on that day. I will forsake them and hide my face from them; they will become easy prey, and many terrible troubles will come upon them.
>
> *Deuteronomy 31:17*

Jeremiah was to tell of the Lord's anger towards the city of Jerusalem and how disaster would come upon it at the hands of the Babylonians:

> For I have set my face against this city for evil and not for good, says the Lord: it shall be given into the hands of the king of Babylon, and he shall burn it with fire.
>
> *Jeremiah 21:10*

- Reflect on a time when you felt God 'looked on you with favour' and a time when you felt he had 'turned his face from you'. How did you feel?
- What did you do?

Isaiah used similar imagery in declaring a better future in which the Lord would save his people:

> In overflowing wrath for a moment I hid my face from you, but with everlasting love I will have compassion on you, says the Lord, your Redeemer.
>
> *Isaiah 54:8*

The smiling, beaming face of God was a sign of blessing:

The Lord spoke to Moses, saying: Speak to Aaron and his
sons, saying, Thus you shall bless the Israelites: You shall
say to them,
The Lord bless you and keep you;
the Lord make his face to shine upon you, and be
gracious to you;
the Lord lift up his countenance upon you, and give
you peace.

Numbers 6:22-6

It still speaks to us today as we hear this blessing used in church
worship.

The Book of Psalms was the 'hymn book' for worship in the
Temple and most of the psalms, if not all, were written for
corporate use. However, as countless Christians throughout the
ages have discovered, the psalms are also powerful expressions
of individual spirituality. Many of them address God in
immediately personal terms, and his attitude towards the
worshipper is keenly felt. The hidden face or the shining face of
God features in many of the psalms. The distraught worshipper
experiences the absence of God – the God who has turned his
face away, hidden his face – and his anguish is obvious: 'How
long, O Lord? Will you forget me for ever? How long will you
hide your face from me?' (Psalm 13:1; see also Psalm 102:2). At
worst it is as though God is hiding his face, not showing favour,
cutting the psalmist off from life itself: 'Do not hide your face
from me, or I shall be like those who go down to the Pit'
(Psalm 143:7). In times of difficulty the worshipper continues
to have trust in God but pleads for deliverance:

> But I trust in you, O Lord;
> I say, 'You are my God.'
> My times are in your hand;
> deliver me from the hand of my enemies and persecutors.
> Let your face shine upon your servant;
> save me in your steadfast love.
>
> *Psalm 31:14-16; see also Psalm 69:16-18*

When a person looks at you, they pay a particular kind of attention. When they pay attention to our best sides it feels fine, but if they are focusing on things that are wrong, we may well wish they would give us less attention, look the other way. This lies behind the plea that God will hide his face from the psalmist's sins: 'Hide your face from my sins, and blot out all my iniquities' (Psalm 51:9). That sense of being the object of God's full attention, which is expressed in terms of God having his face turned towards you, is both an enormous comfort and a privilege. But it is also a possible challenge, especially for those who do wrong: 'The face of the Lord is against evildoers, to cut the remembrance of them from the earth' (Psalm 34:16).

- How much attention do you give to God?
- How often do you seek his face?
- How often do you seek to hide your face from him?

The image of God's face is therefore used to express a whole range of different personal and communal ways about how the presence or absence of God is experienced, whether there is a sense of favour or of dismissal, of closeness or of distance, of loving approval or of judging attention. And this experience of God obviously relates, at least in the way we describe it, to our everyday experiences. My very earliest memory is of being pushed in a pram by my mother. She must have been waiting for someone because she kept walking up and down. For a while she would push the pram and I could see her face. But then she would turn and pull it and her face was hidden. I have no recollection as to why it should have been so, but I do remember this distressed me greatly. It has always given a certain vividness to some of those passages from the Psalms.

A contributor to the *Today* programme on 18 December 2013 stated that loneliness among the elderly, which means they lack regular face-to-face contact with other people, is a greater cause of ill health than a lifetime of smoking. The absence of contact with God is bad for our spiritual health.

b. Eyes

The presence of eyes is no guarantee of the ability to see, either literally or metaphorically. Some people have eyes but are blind. Some can see physically but have no perception, no insight. One of the complaints of the prophets was that the people had eyes but could not see the significance of what was happening, nor perceive the action of God. 'Hear this, O foolish and senseless people, who have eyes, but do not see, who have ears, but do not hear' (Jeremiah 5:21). Blindness was a spiritual and not simply a physical matter.

One of the temptations the snake set before Eve was that eating of the forbidden fruit would mean her eyes would 'be opened', giving her a god-like knowledge, an understanding of good and evil (Genesis 3:5). Eve had no problem with seeing things – indeed, she could see how delightful the fruit was – but it is implied that neither she nor Adam had that deeper insight. There was an innocence about them which God sought to protect. They had the freedom to lose such innocence, and did so in the search for the knowledge of things good and evil, the desire to have their eyes opened.

How a person looks at another can be an indication of what they think of them. Eyes were said to be haughty or proud or evil (Deuteronomy 15:9; 28:54, 56, Authorised Version). Sarai complained to Abram that once her handmaid had conceived, she looked with contempt at her barren mistress: 'I was despised in her eyes' (Genesis 16:5, Authorised Version). In contrast, Ruth was surprised to discover that she found grace in the eyes of her relative Boaz: 'Why have I found favour in your sight, that you should take notice of me, when I am a foreigner?' (Ruth 2:10).

The gods of other religions were often represented as idols having eyes but, as the psalmist declared, this did not mean they could see: 'they have mouths, but do not speak; eyes, but do not see' (Psalm 115:5, also 135:16). Yahweh, on the other hand, was understood by the Hebrews to be a God who could see. Not only did he watch over his creation – 'His eyes are always on [the land], from the beginning of the year to the end of the year' (Deuteronomy 11:12) – but as is indicated earlier in the verse, it was also a caring watch.

He similarly kept an eye on the fortunes, or misdoings, of his people and of the nations:

The Lord looks down from heaven;
he sees all mankind.
From where he sits enthroned he watches
all the inhabitants of the earth –
he who fashions the hearts of them all,
and observes all their deeds.

Psalm 33:13-15

For faithful believers (those who feared the Lord), the Lord would keep a saving eye on them: 'Truly the eye of the Lord is on those who fear him, on those who hope in his steadfast love, to deliver their soul from death, and to keep them alive in famine' (Psalm 33:18, 19). The worshipper believed that by giving God his attention and adoration, by lifting up his eyes to the Lord (Psalm 123:1), the Lord would look favourably upon him, rescue him from danger and protect him in times of trouble (Psalm 141:8).

On the other hand, a prophet like Amos would warn the people that, far from God looking upon them favourably, he would fix his eyes on them 'for harm and not for good' (Amos 9:4). One of the terrible messages that Isaiah was called to deliver at the time of his commissioning was that there would be a time when the people would be unable to see and understand and respond to God, lest they would turn to God and be healed. Judgement had to have its time to take effect:

> Go and say to this people:
> 'Keep listening, but do not comprehend;
> keep looking, but do not understand.'
> Make the mind of this people dull,
> and stop their ears,
> and shut their eyes,
> so that they may not look with their eyes,
> and listen with their ears,
> and comprehend with their minds,
> and turn and be healed.

Isaiah 6:9, 10

The Hebrew religion attempted no image of God, but the concept of the all-seeing eye of God that appears in the symbolism and iconography of a number of other religions (consider the eye of Horus in Egyptian religion, and contemporary Freemasonry) has been represented in some Christian art (such as Supper at Emmaus by Jacopo Pontormo). It derives from the ancient belief found in the Hebrew Scriptures that God observes his creation and therefore knows what is going on, not only on the surface of events but even in the secret recesses of the human heart. This is both a comfort and a threat. That we are never out of God's sight and that there is loving care in his looking out for us reassures us, not least in times of difficulty or anxiety. A sense of the absence of such a watchful, caring God is one way we can experience a time of spiritual darkness.

But like children who have a sense that their parents see everything, not least those things that the children should not be doing, we are aware that there is no hiding from God. Our faults, our failings, our negligence of doing good cannot be hidden from the all-seeing God. We may try to kid others – even kid ourselves – but we cannot kid God. He sees; he knows. Without a belief that there is also forgiveness, we would all be in danger of withering under the weight of having all that we are and do being known by God.

- Does the thought that God is 'all seeing' feel comforting or threatening to you?

c. Ears

If it is true that there are none so blind as those who won't see, then it is equally true that the worst kind of deafness is that which comes from blocking our ears to the truth and to the cries of those in need. The accusation made by God against his people was that they were deaf to his word – 'They have ears, but do not hear (Psalm 115:6; see also Psalm 135:17;

Jeremiah11:8; 17:23; 25:4 and others) – and deaf to the needs of the poor (Isaiah 32:7; Jeremiah 5:28; Ezekiel 22:29). This was evident in the failure of the people to obey God, and in the prevalence of injustice.

However, when Isaiah spoke of the new righteous leader who would emerge from the family of Jesse and on whom the spirit of the Lord would rest (Isaiah 11:1-9), the sign that he would rule justly was that he would not simply depend on what he saw or heard:

> He shall not judge by what his eyes see,
> or decide by what his ears hear;
> but with righteousness he shall judge the poor,
> and decide with equity for the meek of the earth.

Isaiah 11:3, 4

Jesus called those who were open to the meaning of what God was saying to listen and not simply hear: 'Let anyone with ears to hear listen!' (Mark 4:9).

When the psalmist or the prophet spoke of the 'ear' of God, they were most often doing so in the context of worship or individual prayer – of intercession and petition. When the people called upon God, they prayed that he would not be deaf to their cries but 'incline [his] ear' to them (2 Kings 19:16; see also Lamentations 3:56). The righteous could live in the hope that the ears of God would be 'open to their cry' (Psalm 34:15).

In church liturgies, the versicle, 'Lord hear our prayer' and its response, 'and let our cry come unto thee' commonly appear as part of the Intercessions. It is when our calls for help, for ourselves or others, appear to go unanswered that we are most inclined to consider that God is deaf. When the faithful Jew who had gone each day for years to the Western Wall to pray for peace was asked what it felt like since there was no peace, he replied, 'Like talking to a wall.' He's not the only one to have ever felt that.

- How easy do you find it to 'listen' to God?
- Do you have a favourite quiet place where you can be still and wait and listen?

---

d. Mouth

It is natural that we should want God to hear us, to be listening when we pray – not only when we are asking for things but also when we offer thanks, make confession or express our adoration. But the spiritually mature know that their own listening is just as important as speaking, if not more so. It is important to be still, to wait in quietness so that we might hear what God wishes to say to us. It has clearly been a central part of Judaeo/Christian belief that God not only listens but also speaks – he seeks to communicate with his people, to reveal himself and his purposes not only through nature and through action but also through the spoken word.

Creation itself, in the Jewish tradition, is not an act of power but the result of God's speaking. 'Then God said, "Let there be light"; and there was light' (Genesis 1:3). Each of the major acts of creation according to the account in Genesis chapter 1, including the creation of humankind, comes about as a result of God speaking (see also Psalm 33:6). As John says at the beginning of his Gospel, 'In the beginning was the Word . . . All things came into being through him, and without him not one thing came into being' (John 1:1-3).

It is only in the second account of creation in Genesis 2 that there is a more tactile understanding of the creative act. The earth and heavens are 'made' and man is moulded from the dust of the earth. Adam is given life, not by some dramatic act of electric shock, as in the case of the monster Frankenstein, but by God breathing life into Adam – a kind of mouth to mouth suscitation. It is very intimate.

In some passages in the Authorised Version of the Bible, the phrase 'mouth to mouth' is used where modern translations use the phrase 'face to face' (for example, Jeremiah 32:4; 34:3) to convey close proximity between two people.

> • How does it affect your understanding of God that he is a God who 'speaks' and not only 'shows' or 'makes'?

In the books of the Law in the Hebrew Scriptures (the Old Testament), the words from the mouth of God were understood most often as command. What God expected and demanded of his people was spoken to Moses who set down God's ordinances. The Ten Commandments are introduced by, 'Then God spoke all these words' (Exodus 20:1), and 'Moses wrote down all the words of the Lord' (Exodus 24:4). The faithful were those who delighted in God's word ('How sweet are your words to my taste, sweeter than honey to my mouth!' Psalm 119:103) and who treasured in their hearts what the Lord said so that they might do what God required of them ('I treasure your word in my heart, so that I may not sin against you' Psalm 119:11). In words that were to be quoted by Jesus at the time of his temptations, Moses had told the people that bread alone was not enough to give them life, 'but by every word that comes from the mouth of the Lord' (Deuteronomy 8:3).

The word of God could also come as call, as in the case of Samuel (1 Samuel 3:2-14), and as revelation (1 Samuel 3:21). When the prophets spoke in the name of God they understood themselves to be conveying not their own ideas but the words of the Lord. Indeed, it was the promise of God that he would put his words into the mouths of the prophets. Jeremiah experienced it as something tangible: 'Then the Lord put out his hand and touched my mouth; and the Lord said to me, "Now I have put my words in your mouth" ' (Jeremiah 1:9). God was clearly understood to be the source of what they were saying.

When God called Moses to be the leader of his people and told him to tell the people what to do, Moses complained that he was no orator. God replied that Aaron, Moses' brother and a fluent speaker, would be the spokesman:

> You shall speak to him and put the words in his mouth; and I will be with your mouth and with his mouth, and will teach you what you shall do. He indeed shall speak for you to the people; he shall serve as a mouth for you, and you shall serve as God for him.
>
> *Exodus 4:15, 16*

This gives an interesting insight into the way in which the relationship between God and those who spoke in his name was understood.

While Isaiah would tell the people of Jerusalem that the time of their punishment was coming to an end and that God would speak words of comfort to them ('Comfort, O comfort my people, says your God. Speak tenderly to Jerusalem, and cry to her that she has served her term, that her penalty is paid' Isaiah 40:1), there were times when the prophets would have to report harsher things. Hosea spoke of the power of God's words of judgement: 'Therefore I have hewn them by the prophets, I have killed them by the words of my mouth, and my judgement goes forth as the light' (Hosea 6:5).

The power of language in everyday experience makes it easy to understand why there should be this description of revelation as words that come from the mouth of God, revelation understood in terms of what God requires of us and commands of us, how he loves us, how he calls us, and how he communicates his judgement and his compassion. The messages of the lawgivers and the prophets were given authority by the declaration that their words were what the mouth of the Lord had spoken (e.g. Isaiah 1:19, 20; Micah 4:1-4). It was an effective word that, having been spoken, would not return without having achieved its purpose:

> Turn to me and be saved,
> all the ends of the earth!
> For I am God and there is no other.
> By myself have I sworn,
> from my mouth has gone forth in righteousness
> a word that shall not return:
> 'To me every knee shall bow,
> every tongue shall swear.'
>
> *Isaiah 45:22, 23*

The word of God is ultimately a word of salvation.

- In what ways have you heard God 'speak' to you?
- Have they been words of 'guidance', 'call', 'command', 'comfort', 'judgement', 'forgiveness', 'instruction', 'blessing'?

---

e. Hands and arms

The hand is normally the means by which human beings grasp, hold, make, point, touch and manipulate. The possession of an opposable thumb is, depending on which definition is used, unique to human beings or something they have in common with some other primates. The hand has the ability to be used with either delicate tenderness or violent aggression. To be open-handed is a sign of generosity; to be tight-fisted a sign of meanness. The outstretched hand may indicate welcome; the raised hand can be a show of anger. The French are said to 'speak with their hands', and certainly the hands are vital in systems such as British Sign Language for communication with deaf people. The hands can be the means of betrayal, as when we 'hand someone over', or a sign of practical involvement – 'hands on'. The Free Dictionary suggests almost 200 different idioms featuring 'hands'. They clearly play a significant part in our behaviour and relationships.

Although the account of creation in Genesis 1 indicates that God created by the power of his word, elsewhere the preference is for a more direct description in terms of God's making by the power of his hand. Isaiah, for example, speaks of the heavens being 'stretched out' by God's hands (Isaiah 45:12), and that human beings are the 'work of [his] hand', like clay in the hand of the potter (Isaiah 64:8). Job witnessed to his dependence on God in that it was God's hands that had made him (Job 10:8). The psalmist celebrated God's creative action: 'In his hand are the depths of the earth; the heights of the mountains are his also. The sea is his, for he made it, and the dry land, which his hands have formed' (Psalm 95:4, 5).

> • What different insights do you gain from the descriptions of God's act of creating through 'command' and those through 'making and moulding'?

We, and all creation, are in this sense part of God's 'handiwork'. Creating was God's work, and the implication in Genesis is that it took effort, for at the end of the six days of creating God 'rested' (Genesis 2:2, 3). This was to be reflected in the command to keep that day of God's rest as a day of rest for people as well (Deuteronomy 5:12-15; Exodus 34:21; 35:2, 3). But that didn't mean God did not continue to be active (see John 5:17: 'My Father is still working . . .').

As far as creation was concerned, it was understood that it was by God's goodness and action that the creation was sustained. It was by the generous, open-handedness of God that the animal kingdom was not only fed but filled: 'These [creatures] all look to you to give them their food in due season; when you give to them, they gather it up; when you open your hand, they are filled with good things' (Psalm 104:27, 28).

An effective god has to be a god who does things, achieves things, acts on behalf of his followers. A god who can but won't, who could but doesn't, is of little use. To put it in everyday terms, a god who sits on his hands is ineffective. The Hebrews believed that their God was an active God, and this was often expressed in terms of his having a 'strong hand' and a hand stretched out to accomplish his purposes. God's action in the people's escape from Egypt was highly significant in the tradition of the Hebrews, and the Exodus became a foundational event in their history. It was a powerful reminder to the people that their God was a God of effective and saving action.

> - What kind of prayers do you feel are appropriate in a time of conflict when servicemen and women from your country are involved?

Moses went to Pharaoh to warn him of the plagues that would strike the country at the hand of God:

> Then the Lord said to Moses, 'Rise up early in the morning and present yourself before Pharaoh, and say to him "Thus says the Lord, the God of the Hebrews: Let my people go so that they may worship me. For this time I will send all my plagues upon you yourself, and upon your officials, and upon your people, so that you may know that there is no one like me in all the earth. For by now I could have stretched out my hand and struck you and your people with pestilence, and you would have been cut off from the earth." '
>
> *Exodus 9:13-15*

Such action was itself proof that the God of the Hebrews was more powerful and more effective than the gods of other nations. Later, when the people had safely escaped from Egypt, Moses commanded them to remember the event: 'Remember this day on which you came out of Egypt, out of the house of slavery, because the Lord brought you out from there by strength of hand' (Exodus 13:3; see also 13:9). Yahweh's hand was powerful in attacking the nations who were enemies of the Hebrews, and effective in saving his people.

The arm provides extension for the hand – it gives it reach. The arm is most often used as a description of powerful action. For Jeremiah it was the Lord's arm outstretched in creating that was evidence of his power to do all things: 'Ah Lord God! It is you who made the heavens and the earth by your outstretched arm! Nothing is too hard for you' (Jeremiah 32:17). But, as we have already seen, it was in God's saving action in bringing the Hebrew people out of Egypt that his power was most evident. In the Pentateuch (the first five books of the Old Testament), the images of the mighty hand and the outstretched arm are often brought together – for example:

> 'I am the Lord and I will free you from the burdens of the Egyptians and deliver you from slavery to them. I will redeem you with an outstretched arm and with mighty acts of judgement.'
>
> *Exodus 6:6;*
> *see also Deuteronomy 4:34; 5:15; 11:2; Psalm 77:15*

Moses saw the Exodus as proof that Yahweh was superior to any other god, for no other god had achieved such an amazing rescue act:

> 'Has any god ever attempted to go and take a nation for himself from the midst of another nation, by trials, by signs and wonders, by war, by a mighty hand and an outstretched arm, and by terrifying displays of power, as the Lord your God did for you in Egypt before your very eyes?'
>
> *Deuteronomy 4:34*

If an effective hand or arm was 'outstretched', then a hand 'shortened' was a sign of ineffectiveness. Isaiah reports the Lord as complaining to his people, 'Why did no one answer when I called? Is my hand shortened, that it cannot redeem? Or have I no power to deliver? (Isaiah 50:2). And later he was to tell the people that far from it being God's lack of power to save them, it was their sinfulness that had created a block between them and their God:

See, the Lord's hand is not too short to save,
nor his ear too dull to hear.
Rather, your iniquities have been barriers
between you and your God,
and your sins have hidden his face from you
so that he does not hear.

Isaiah 59:1, 2

- In what ways have you seen God's hand being 'outstretched'?
- What events would you describe as occasions when God's hand was 'shortened'?

The action of God was not only understood in terms of the life and fortunes of the nation but also in the way in which he influenced the lives of individuals. Job had good reason to feel that God was active in his life – both for good and for ill. Satan had challenged God to test Job by bringing him ill fortune:

> Then Satan answered the Lord, 'Does Job fear God for nothing? Have you not put a fence around him and his house and all that he has, on every side? You have blessed the work of his hands, and his possessions have increased in the land. But stretch out your hand now, and touch all that he has, and he will curse you to your face.'
>
> *Job 1:9-11; see also 2:5*

Job recognised that he had been made by God but bewailed the way God was now treating him: 'Your hands fashioned and made me; and now you turn and destroy me. Remember that you fashioned me like clay; and will you turn me to dust again?' (Job 10:8, 9).

Naomi, too, saw the loss of her husband and her two sons as the result of God's action. As she told Orpah and Ruth, her daughters-in-law, 'No, my daughters, it has been far more bitter for me than for you, because the hand of the Lord has turned against me' (Ruth 1:13).

Others experienced God in a more benign way, as a God whose care stretched to the furthest parts: 'If I take the wings of the morning and settle at the farthest limits of the sea, even there your hand shall lead me, and your right hand shall hold me fast' (Psalm 139:9, 10). Elsewhere the psalmist spoke of God as a saving God and in whose hands one would feel secure: 'Into your hand I commit my spirit; you have redeemed me, O Lord, faithful God' (Psalm 31:5). Such a confidence was, according to St Luke, heard in Jesus' final utterance on the cross, offsetting the deeply disturbing earlier cry of forsakenness: 'Father, into your hands I commend my spirit' (Luke 23:46).

God's arms, too, were seen to be supportive, as in Psalm 89:21 where David was promised the strength of God's arm, and in Isaiah 33:2 where the people asked that, in times of trouble, they would experience the saving power of God's arm each morning. As shepherd, the Lord would feed his people and keep the little ones safe: 'He will feed his flock like a shepherd; he will gather the lambs in his arms' (Isaiah 40:11). In giving his farewell blessing to the people of Israel, Moses declared that they would find security in God and be supported by his everlasting arms: 'The eternal God is your refuge and underneath are the everlasting arms' (Deuteronomy 33:27 NIV, but note the alternative translation in the NRSV: 'He subdues the ancient gods, shatters the forces of old'). The sense that they are held secure in God's embrace has been a comfort to many people throughout the ages, and this verse has provided the text for many sermons in difficult times.

Our more sceptical age is often reticent about ascribing events on the international scene or in the lives of individuals as being directly attributable to the action of God. In times of war there may be the desire to believe that God is on one's own side, and prayers offered both by nations and by individuals can call for God to be active in support of them, both to achieve victory and to keep safe. But as the complexity of international relations are more widely broadcast and understood, prayers can seek to reflect a more complex understanding of the way God might be called upon to act. It is less easy to assume that right simply abides with 'us' and that we can therefore assume God's support.

Similarly, a better understanding and knowledge of the sciences, even at the popular level, informs how we think about the way our world and we ourselves work. We are less ready to assume that a natural disaster or a personal tragedy is the result of God's action. We are more likely to assume that such things occur as the result of global weather systems or the activity of biochemical interactions.

For some people, this simply means that they no longer believe in God at all, or that his effective action is so reduced as to relegate him to a private world of generalised spirituality. The manipulative, interfering God is seen, even by firm believers, as a God they have rejected. For such people, God's activity has to be understood in a much more subtle and theologically sophisticated way that acknowledges both a God at work within his creation and a creation that enjoys the opportunities and responsibilities of considerable freedom. For them it is not nonsense to speak of God's hand being seen in events, but such language is only felt to make sense, and to be true to our experience and our knowledge, if it takes into account the relative independence of creation within its ultimate dependence upon God.

Of course, there will also be Christians who feel no need for such reticence. For them, theological sophistication is seen as sophistry and as a denial of faith in a God whose past activity is testified to in the Scriptures and whose promises continue to be played out through his actions here and now. They are happy to declare that their personal experience echoes the witness of those who announced that the hand of God was upon them, the hand of God had touched them.

Before we too readily applaud one group and condemn the other (whichever group that might be), we might consider that there are truths to which each of them is seeking to be faithful. The Christian faith centres on a God who in his outgoing love does things: creates, sustains, forgives, judges, nurtures, welcomes, rescues. To view events and our own lives without seeking and perceiving God's involvement is to impoverish the rich complexity of the ways things are. It is to deny the nature of the God we claim to follow. But the way we seek to describe that involvement must not ignore the reality of the world – the material world we learn more and more about every year – for that very world is God's world, the world he loves and for which Jesus sacrificed everything. The search for truth is not to be restrained by a falsely restrictive spirituality as though it protects God from understandings that leave him less and less room within which to operate. God needs no such protection from us, however well-meaning our intentions.

> • In what terms do you seek to describe the activity of God in the world of nature and in the lives of men and women?

f. Feet

In the Van Eyck altar piece there are shoes on God's feet. As was noted in the introduction, this is considered to be indicative of the fact that the figure is that of God the Father – Christ is more normally depicted unshod. It is also a sign of status. Here is the ruler, a person whose importance is being emphasised rather than his humility. In the presence of the Holy, Moses was commanded to remove his sandals, to go barefoot.

To be under someone's foot was to be subject to them or even subjugated by them. The psalmist declared that God had put everything under the control of human beings: 'You have given them dominion over the works of your hands; you have put all things under their feet' (Psalm 8:6). More dramatically, this could be a matter of being trampled on. The king (David?) was promised that God would protect him and enable him to put down all his enemies: 'You will tread on the lion and the adder, the young lion and the serpent you will trample under foot' (Psalm 91:13). Isaiah used a vivid and violent image in describing the action of God in enacting vengeance over Edom and vindication for Zion:

> I have trodden the wine press alone,
> and from the peoples no one was with me . . .
> their juice spattered on my garments,
> and stained all my robes . . .
> I trampled down peoples in my anger,
> I crushed them in my wrath,
> and I poured out their lifeblood on the earth.
> (Isaiah 63:3, 6)

See also the psalmist's plea to God to show his power: 'Trample under foot those who lust after tribute' (Psalm 68:30).

If the hands and the arms were symbolic of the strength and effectiveness of God, it might have been assumed that the feet would speak of the speed with which the action was carried out. We speak of being 'fleet of foot', both literally and metaphorically, and to 'drag your feet' is indicative of tardy effort. However, very little use is made of the image of the feet with reference to God.

- Why do you think God's feet are so seldom referred to, especially when compared with descriptions of his arms and hands?

---

g. Roles

The use of imagery based on parts of the human body is but one aspect of a more general anthropomorphic way of describing God. Descriptions of God's status, ways of relating to his creation, his activity and his attitudes are also frequently given in terms of human roles. In some instances it is obvious that this way of describing God is by way of an extended simile.

King

The Scriptures give evidence of some ambivalence around the creation of the monarchy – it is a sign of the people's failure to trust God and yet Samuel anoints Saul on the instructions of God. At heart, Israel was a theocracy – ruled by God as their king. The earthly ruler was in that sense God's 'regent', his anointed, his 'son' even (see Psalm 2:7). The king had the ruler's power and status; he could command the people and have a standing army to lead into battle for the protection of the nation and for defence against its enemies. But there was also the understanding that it was in fact God who was their ruler, their king, the leader of Israel's armies, the one who fought in Israel's defence and who gained victories: 'You are my King and my God; you command victories for Jacob' (Psalm 44:4).

While a change of earthly ruler could bring instability, internecine fighting and an uncertain future, the people could look to God as an unchanging power. As the psalmist says, 'The Lord is king for ever and ever' (Psalm 10:16); 'The Lord sits enthroned as king for ever' (Psalm 29:10). Jeremiah would also affirm that 'the Lord is the true God; he is the living God and the everlasting King' (Jeremiah 10:10). Not only was he the king over the nation of Israel, their protector God; he was also king over all the earth and all the nations:

> For the Lord, the Most High, is awesome,
> a great king over all the earth . . .
> Sing praises to God, sing praises;
> sing praises to our King, sing praises.
> For God is the king of all the earth . . .
> God is king over the nations.
>
> *Psalm 47:2, 6-8*

More than that, he was also king over the other gods, those who protected and ruled the other nations: 'For the Lord is a great God, and a King above all gods' (Psalm 95:3).

Belief in the sovereignty of God was reinforced and displayed in ritual worship, most obviously in the processional celebrations of the enthronement of the monarch and the annual Ingathering and Tabernacles festivals at the turn of the year when God's epiphany and enthronement were celebrated. This can be seen in the Psalms, the 'hymn book' of the Temple, where some 40 psalms reflect this event – for example, 'Your solemn processions are seen, O God, the processions of my God, my King, into the sanctuary' (Psalm 68:24). These annual celebrations also reflected the occasion when David had the ark taken to Jerusalem. Antiphonal chants used on such occasions are found in Psalm 24, where the reference to the 'heads' of the gates may have been an actual upper part of the gate structure that needed to be lifted to allow the ark of the Lord to pass through:

> Lift up your heads, O gates!
> and be lifted up, O ancient doors!
> that the King of glory may come in.
> Who is the King of glory?
> The Lord strong and mighty,
> the Lord, mighty in battle.
> Lift up your heads, O gates!
> and be lifted up, O ancient doors!
> that the King of glory may come in.
> Who is the King of glory?
> The Lord of hosts,
> he is the King of glory.

Psalm 24:7-10

Similar titles are afforded God in a more individual psalm of longing: 'Even the sparrow finds a home, and the swallow a nest for herself, where she may lay her young, at your altars, O Lord of hosts, my King and my God' (Psalm 84:3), and in David's outpouring of praise: 'I will extol you, my God and King, and bless your name for ever and ever' (Psalm 145:1).

In Isaiah's account of his call it is noticeable that once again we are in the context of a Temple celebration and a time of uncertainty – it was the year in which King Uzziah died. Isaiah's vision of the Lord on his throne, high and lifted up, attended by the heavenly court of seraphim, makes the prophet acutely aware of his own unworthiness: 'Woe is me! I am lost, for I am a man of unclean lips, and I live among a people of unclean lips; yet my eyes have seen the King, the Lord of hosts!' (Isaiah 6:5).

In his grief for the people, Jeremiah not only identified with their plight and the distress that confronted them, but he also joined in their question of where God was in it all: 'Hark, the cry of my poor people from far and wide in the land: "Is the Lord not in Zion? Is her King not in her?" ' (Jeremiah 8:19). The sense of loss of the presence of God as King of Israel, present in Zion, added to the overall uncertainty and fear in time of trouble. In a more positive mood, the prophet could declare, 'But the Lord is the true God; he is the living God and the everlasting King' (Jeremiah 10:10). Such an affirmation pervades the prophet's sense that the fortunes of the people are in the power and under the rule of God, whether that be for punishment of their sins or salvation from disaster.

Shepherd

Most people recognise, of course, that although the psalmist describes God as a shepherd (Psalm 23:1), God does not actually have a crook and a flock of sheep, even though his people are sometimes called his flock. The image is attempting to capture just something of the way God is experienced both by individuals and by the people as a whole: that God looks after his people, protects them, ensures they have resources of food and water, are sheltered in times of adversity, and fights off those who would harm them. God is the leader of his people, guiding them and meeting their needs.

In troubled times, when the people longed to be saved, the psalmist called upon God as Israel's shepherd, beseeching him to save them: 'Give ear, O Shepherd of Israel, you who lead Joseph like a flock! . . . Stir up your might, and come to save us!' (Psalm 80:1, 2).

In a country where a flock was precious and could constitute the major part of a family's wealth, the role of the shepherd was important. Isaiah gave hope to the people by depicting the Lord God coming to them as a powerful figure but with the care of a shepherd:

See, the Lord God comes with might,
and his arm rules for him . . .
He will feed his flock like a shepherd;
he will gather the lambs in his arms,
and carry them in his bosom,
and gently lead the mother sheep.

Isaiah 40:10, 11

- How suitable do you feel it is to refer to God as 'shepherd' these days?
- Is there a different image that might be more relevant in today's world?

Kings were likened to shepherds and expected to show the caring qualities of shepherds. One of the worst things for the nation was to be without an effective leader, and when Micaiah sought to show the king just how dire the situation for the people would be, he said he saw Israel scattered on the mountain like sheep without a shepherd (1 Kings 22:17). Bad rulers were sometimes described as bad shepherds, and when the Lord, through the prophet Jeremiah, wished to make clear the disaster he was bringing upon the people, it was the plight of the rulers that he emphasised: 'Wail, you shepherds, and cry out; roll in ashes, you lords of the flock, for the days of your slaughter have come' (Jeremiah 25:34).

Ezekiel uttered an extended prophecy against the rulers of Israel in terms of the Lord's complaint against them as bad shepherds of his flock: 'Ah, you shepherds of Israel who have been feeding yourselves! Should not shepherds feed the sheep?' (Ezekiel 34:2). And having railed against them, the Lord said that he would take upon himself the task of shepherding his sheep:

> As shepherds seek out their flocks when they are among their scattered sheep, so I will seek out my sheep. I will rescue them from all the places to which they have been scattered on a day of clouds and thick darkness.
>
> *Ezekiel 34:12*

Jesus used the image of the 'good shepherd' as a sign of the leadership and care he would exercise over his followers (John 10:11).

It is intriguing that while the use of the shepherd image normally has positive associations, the reputation of those who actually tended sheep is generally bad. Indeed, shepherding was viewed in the time of Jesus as 'unclean', and the Pharisees would have considered shepherds as 'sinners' – a term used not only to denote those who lived immoral lives but also to refer to those who followed a proscribed trade or profession, such as prostitutes. There is therefore a discrepancy between the generally noble view of shepherds that is seen in the Old Testament and the rabbinic view that was current in the first century AD. How this came about is not clear.

In addition to this we might note that in the Gospel account it was shepherds, out in the fields, who were first told of the birth of Christ (Luke 2:8-20). Is this the Gospel writer's way of saying that the Messiah was for 'sinners', perhaps especially for sinners, and not just for the righteous? Further, Jesus' parable of the lost sheep (Luke 15:1-7) was provocatively addressed to the Pharisees as though they themselves were shepherds: 'And the Pharisees and the scribes were grumbling and saying, "This fellow welcomes sinners and eats with them." So he told them this parable: Which one of you . . . ?" ' This can be viewed as an attack by Jesus on the Pharisaic attitude towards proscribed trades and reflects his own position in terms of how he welcomed sinners.[4]

Father, Mother

Christians are used to following Jesus' example in calling God 'Father' (or more precisely 'Daddy'), but the use of 'Father' for God is rare in the Old Testament. The authority titles of King and Lord are frequent, but not the more intimate, parental name. This may in part be accounted for by the presence of religions in nations around Israel that made use of much more sexual imagery in describing the activity of their gods and which was expressed through the cultic rituals in their temples, such as through temple prostitutes. While Israel was not immune to the attraction of such religions, the orthodoxy set out in the Mosaic law and the message of the prophets made it clear that this was against Yahweh's commandments. Father, as an honorific title, was used for the Patriarchs like Abraham, or for a king, but seldom for God. This was not because the Hebrews had no concept of God's care for them – far from it – but such care and compassion were usually expressed through the use of other imagery, such as shepherd. However, reference to God as Father is not totally absent, and the psalmist uses it to emphasise the care of God for his people, especially the vulnerable: 'Father of orphans and protector of widows is God

---

4. See Kenneth E. Bailey, *Poet and Peasant* and *Through Peasant Eyes*, combined edition (Grand Rapids: Eerdmans, 1983).

in his holy habitation' (Psalm 68:5); 'As a father has compassion for his children, so the Lord has compassion for those who fear him. For he knows how we were made; he remembers that we are dust' (Psalm 103:13, 14). One of the expected responsibilities of the monarch was that he would have care of the vulnerable.

As we have seen above, the king was sometimes spoken of as God's son, and in Psalm 89, which celebrates the covenant made with David, it is stated that the king 'shall cry to me, "You are my Father, my God, and the Rock of my salvation!" ' (Psalm 89:26). The people, too, according to Isaiah, would call upon God as Father: 'You, O Lord, are our father; our Redeemer from of old is your name' (Isaiah 63:16b).

God's complaint about Israel was that although he had expected them to look to him as a father, obediently following him, they had in fact proved to be faithless:

'And I thought you would call me, My Father,
and would not turn from following me.
Instead, as a faithless wife leaves her husband,
so you have been faithless to me, O house of Israel.'

Jeremiah 3:19, 20

The disobedient children suffered the punishment of the father in that they were taken into exile in a strange land. In bringing his people back from exile, it was as though the Lord would again become father to his people who had endured separation from their homeland like fatherless children: 'See I am going to bring them from the land of the north, and gather them from the farthest parts of the earth . . . for I have become a father to Israel, and Ephraim is my firstborn' (Jeremiah 31:8, 9). God's care for his children was even greater than that of a woman for her baby: 'Can a woman forget her nursing-child, or show no compassion for the child of her womb? Even these may forget, yet I will not forget you' (Isaiah 49:15).

In the New Testament the role of God as Father is emphasised through Jesus' typical reference to God as his Father and the way in which Jesus was understood to be uniquely God's Son. In fact, it is so embedded in the Christian understanding of God that there is a temptation to forget that in using these descriptions we are still using imagery as ways of talking about the intimate and indeed unique relationship within the Godhead. They are not 'biological' descriptions, although the way in which the account of the Virgin birth is sometimes understood can encourage such a mistake.

- What aspects of your relationship with God would you understand as best being described by referring to God as 'Father'?
- Would the term 'Mother' enrich that description? If so, what would it add?

Chapter two
Jesus

Few people today would doubt the historical existence of a man called Jesus, a Jew born around the time of the end of King Herod's reign and who became an itinerant preacher known for his healings and exorcisms, who was famous for his stories that conveyed his understanding of God, who had a wide following as well as an inner group of disciples and who died at the hands of the Romans by crucifixion. But it is what is believed about him that is most significant and which led his followers to worship him as equal to God.

Followers like St Paul and the later Fathers of the Church set out to explain the significance of Jesus' life, death and resurrection and sought to understand his humanity and divinity and the relationship between them. In Jewish terms there was the discussion as to whether or not he was the promised and long-expected Messiah, the Anointed One of God who would herald the coming of God's kingdom and rule. He may have called himself the Son of Man – possibly as a way of avoiding the sacred title 'I am' or as a way of declaring himself to be a representative not only of Israel but of humanity – but he appears to have been reticent about using the greater title 'Son of God'.

In seeking to ensure orthodoxy among the increasingly scattered communities of Christians from Gentile as well as Jewish backgrounds, it was necessary to provide agreed formulations by which to describe Jesus. In doing so, use was made of terms from Greek philosophy – as, for example, in the later credal statements that speak of 'substance', 'person' and 'essence'. St Matthew's account of Jesus' conception and birth offered one way of setting out his uniqueness and was the basis for long arguments about just how he could be understood to be both fully human and fully divine. His uniqueness was in part conveyed by the concept that while he was not 'made' by God, he was 'begotten' of God the Holy Spirit and (or 'through') the Virgin Mary. Those who believed he was not fully human but only appeared to be (Docetists), as well as those who believed he was not eternally divine (such as Adoptionists), were considered to be heretics even though they appealed to the New Testament to support their views.

It is Christian orthodoxy to believe that Jesus was fully human – although that is still modified by the phrase 'yet without sin' (Hebrews 4:15). There have always been attempts to idealise this. In art and in sculpture Jesus' spiritual perfection has sometimes been reflected in a portrayal of physical perfection. The Christmas carol 'Away in a manger' implies a perfect baby – 'no crying he makes'.[5] Some theologians believe that Jesus' knowledge was perfect but that he chose to hide his knowledge.

The Gospels give us very few details about his growing up. There is just one story in Luke 2:41-51 concerning the 12-year-old boy's visit to Jerusalem, and it is Luke also who says that 'Jesus increased in wisdom and in years' (or 'stature', NIV) (Luke 2:52). There is no contemporary picture or description of Jesus' physical appearance. All portraits are works of imagination. So although there is no doubt about his physical presence, some care is needed in speaking about his body, where the focus of attention is not upon appearance but upon significance; not upon what his body was like but upon what it meant. To this extent, references to Jesus' various physical attributes are used as evocative images conveying theological rather than biological points.

---

5. Charles H. Gabriel, 'Away in a manger' (1856–1932) (Public Domain).

a. Head

What a person looks like is focused in the head. Features are, of course, not the whole story, and in themselves tell little about a person's height, stature or body type, all of which are important. But it is the features that provide the usual indication of a person's identity. Recently, attempts have been made by forensic scientists and artists to recreate what Jesus may have looked like in terms of his ethnic, racial type. The result is, of course, more generalised than specific, but at least it goes some way to correcting the ingrained and unconscious assumption in the white Western world that Jesus had the appearance of an Anglo Saxon! Those who believe that ancient Hebrews and Jews of Jesus' time were, in fact, black would say that these attempts have not gone far enough and that images of Jesus still harbour attitudes of white and Arab supremacy. Clearly, the matter has strong political overtones. And the Bible provides no conclusive evidence other than making it clear that Jesus was a Jew. The Gospel writers had no interest in describing what he looked like. Their concern was what he did and what he was.

This lack of descriptive information has both advantages and disadvantages. A possible disadvantage is that because we do not know just what Jesus looked like, there can be a temptation to underplay the very particularity of Jesus and so lose something of his humanity. Rather than a particular man he becomes a theological construct in human form. On the other hand, as the 'Man for others' (all others), the universal 'saviour', the lack of specific details about his features means that he can be imaged in the way that meets our needs. In this sense it is just as right for him to be pictured as white as it is for him to be black, as right to be brown as it is to be yellow, since he is the saviour of all races, all colours, all ethnic groups, all sorts and conditions. It is when these images are used as a propaganda tool in the sphere of power politics that they can become destructive.

Quite apart from providing key aspects of a person's appearance, the head is powerfully symbolic. In some instances it can, as it were, stand for the whole person. The Gospels record that when someone came up to Jesus declaring that he would follow Jesus wherever he went, Jesus replied, 'Foxes have holes, and birds of the air have nests; but the Son of Man has nowhere to lay his head' (Matthew 8:20; Luke 9:57, 58). As well as the reference to the world of nature in which even birds and animals have places to rest, there may have been a political overtone in what Jesus said. The birds symbolised Gentiles and the foxes certain foreigners who were political enemies of Israel. In a hidden, symbolic way, Jesus may have been saying that in the land of Palestine, the Romans had seized their place, as also had Herod, a king seen by Jews as a foreigner and described by Jesus on another occasion as 'that fox' (Luke 13:32). But the Son of Man, the 'true Israel', had no place. To follow Jesus meant being disinherited rather than being assured a position of security and influence. That was the challenge to the would-be disciple.

We talk of 'head teachers', the 'head of a corporation', 'headquarters'. The word conveys importance, seniority, status, power. In the Epistles, Jesus is described as 'head over all things' (Ephesians 1:22) and 'the head of the church' (Ephesians 5:23; Colossians 1:18). Conversely, the bowing of the head is a sign of humility, of acknowledging another person's status. Courtiers bow their head before the monarch, and worshippers in church will sometimes bow their head at key points in the liturgy – such as at the mention of the name of Jesus, at the reference to the incarnation in the creed ('and became man') or when approaching the altar. This double symbolic meaning – of status and of humility – is seen in two key instances in the story of Jesus: the anointing of his head by the woman (Mark 14:3) and the placing of a crown of thorns on his head prior to his crucifixion (Matthew 27:29).

The practice of anointing with oil as a means of dedicating has a long history. Objects used in religious rituals were often consecrated by having oil poured over them, and instructions were given for the production of the holy oil used in the ceremony of consecration (see Exodus 29, 30). The heads of priests like Aaron and his sons, or of kings like Saul and David, were anointed as a way of consecrating them for their duties and responsibilities (Exodus 30:30; 1 Samuel 9:16; 15:1; 2 Samuel 2:4). The action of anointing the king is recorded in Psalm 45:7, a psalm for a royal wedding. Isaiah believed himself to be 'anointed' by the Lord for his ministry: 'The spirit of the Lord God is upon me, because the Lord has anointed me; he has sent me to bring good news to the oppressed' (Isaiah 61:1).

Jesus was believed to have been uniquely the one anointed by God. The Greek title Christ means 'anointed' and is a translation of the Hebrew equivalent Messiah. In Luke's Gospel Jesus is understood to have identified himself with the one referred to in the Isaiah passage mentioned above. In the rejoicing at the release of Peter and John, their friends tell of how

> both Herod and Pontius Pilate, with the Gentiles and the peoples of Israel, gathered together against your [God's] holy servant Jesus, whom you anointed, to do whatever your hand and your plan had predestined to take place.
>
> *Acts 4:27, 28*

When the woman came into the room where Jesus was being entertained by Simon the leper she broke open her jar of ointment and poured it over Jesus' head as an act of anointing (Mark14:3-9). Luke and John give alternative accounts of this act (Luke 7:36-50; John 12:1-8) and state that the oil was poured over his feet, not his head (see Feet below). Some of those present at the supper scolded the woman, seeing her action as a waste, but Jesus commended her: 'Let her alone; why do you trouble her? She has performed a good service for me . . . She has done what she could; she has anointed my body beforehand for its burial.' This is a further instance of where the head symbolises the whole body. While Jesus' reference is to the anointing of the body of a dead person (here performed beforehand), the Gospel writers may equally have had in mind the anointing of a king, thus indicating that Jesus' kingship could only be realised through his death. This brought together the two themes of his kingly status and his humiliating end.

After his arrest Jesus was subjected not only to an unjust trial but also to humiliating abuse from the soldiers in charge of him. They no doubt saw it as a piece of horseplay, the legitimate fun soldiers could have at the expense of their prisoners. As recorded in the Gospels it is full of irony:

> Then the soldiers led him into the courtyard of the palace (that is, the governor's headquarters); and they called together the whole cohort. And they clothed him in a purple cloak; and after twisting some thorns in a crown, they put it on him And they began saluting him, 'Hail, King of the Jews!' They struck his head with a reed, spat upon him, and knelt down in homage to him.
>
> *Mark 15:16-19*

This is echoed in the sign that Pilate had nailed over Jesus' head on the cross: 'Jesus of Nazareth, the King of the Jews' (John 19:19).

And so through both an anointing and a crowning, the twin threads of Christ's kingly status and his humiliation through mockery and death are brought together. In the Christian tradition it is after the resurrection and ascension that the full nature of Christ's royal authority was revealed. As Thomas Kelly's hymn proclaims:

The head that once was crowned with thorns
Is crowned with glory now.[6]

b. Hands

Jesus was known as the carpenter, the son of a carpenter, although the word used may indicate a more general manual worker. Whatever he did, he knew what it was to work with his hands – to handle the very physicality of materials, the weight of a hammer, the feel of the grain. His were the rough hands of a worker that had bled when a chisel slipped and were calloused from the constant wear and tear. They were 'doing' hands, a man's hands, yet with a tenderness of touch that could reassure, welcome, heal and save. When he returned to his home town after building a reputation as a preacher and healer, the villagers were amazed at what he had been doing, what his hands had been achieving far in excess of his carpentry: 'What deeds of power are done by his hands! Is this not the carpenter, the son of Mary and brother of James and Joses and Judas and Simon, and are not his sisters here with us?' (Mark 6:2). He was not just a woodworker; he was also a marvel worker, and the people could hardly credit it.

For our own reasons and from a quite different world viewpoint, we still find it difficult to credit it. We speak of miracles, although it is not a word that appears in the Gospels. Believers have tended to see in miracles proof of a supernatural action from 'beyond'. But this is not how they would have been understood at the time of Jesus. Rather they would

---

6. Thomas Kelly, 'The head that once was crowned with thorns' (1769–1854) (Public Domain).

have been seen as divine activity within creation in ways that were not necessarily expected. That Jesus did do some remarkable things, especially healings, is now generally agreed, although there is less emphasis upon the events as miracles proving his divinity, and more on the meaning and purpose of the events in bringing in the kingdom.

We sometimes say that we are touched by others – by the pathos of their story, the wonder of their success against the odds, the vitality of their creative imagination. And no doubt Jesus touched many in this way by the power of his teaching, the depth of his spiritual integrity or the selflessness he exhibited. But he also literally touched them – often when others felt he should have kept clear. We see this especially in his healing ministry.

Evidence from the community of Jews at Qumran indicates that, among some Jews at least, to have certain disabilities meant you were no longer a full member of the Jewish community, the people of God. This was true not only of those suffering from leprosy – a group that has been ostracised by many communities over the years – but also of anyone who suffered any kind of blemish – the blind, the deaf, the lame, the dumb. They were not viewed as true Israelites. They were considered to be ritually unclean – as was the woman with the 'issue of blood' and the crippled woman whom Satan had bound (Luke 8:43-8; 13:16). To touch them would render unclean that person also – as indeed would touching the body of a dead person.

Jesus seemed to go out of his way to touch the untouchable. He did so because he sought to bring them shalom, 'wholeness' which was not simply a matter of healing them from their disease, but also of restoration to their place as members of the people of Israel. Making a person 'whole' wasn't just a question of healing a physical condition; it also involved personal well-being, ritual cleanness, a place back in society. The wholeness was to do with a person's individual well-being, their acceptance in a religious community and their place among the people of God.

There are always corporate and communal implications to both sickness and health, to sin and salvation, to disease and wholeness. In touching those who were ritually unclean, Jesus risked being declared unclean himself. It was therefore a radical action that could be justified only by the results – his entering into the position of the ostracised in order to restore them. Jesus' ministry of healing was at one with, and was symbolic of, his whole ministry of restoration and transformation – a ministry to bring 'salvation' within the kingdom of the Father. He placed himself in the human place, the place of separation, in order to bring all people to the place of at-one-ment with God, the place of individual restoration, the place of religious acceptance, the place of community among the people of God.

> - What illnesses do you think still have a social stigma attached to them?
> - What might churches do to help overcome this?

There are accounts of Jesus conducting healings when there were crowds of people around – and equally accounts of times when he withdrew either because of hostility, a lack of faith or, no doubt, his own exhaustion. But the more detailed accounts draw attention to what the sickness and disease of individuals say about the human condition: its failure to see the signs of the times and the coming of the kingdom; its failure to hear with understanding the message of God's rule, his activity, his invitation; its failure to act and to walk in God's way because it is paralysed by guilt and fear, by regulation and false values; its failure to speak out for justice and compassion; its failure to live well because it is overcome by the false spirits of an evil age. When Jesus reached out and touched people with healing he was, in the understanding of the time, taking on the condition of the human heart that was in danger of being enslaved to evil; he was battling against the powers of darkness and wrong, of unfaithfulness and betrayal. His healing was a physical matter but also a deeply spiritual one. They were telling examples of the deeds of power done by his hand.

Understanding disease as signs of the work of the Evil One is not at all the same as saying that the individuals themselves were evil. Jesus resisted such a simplistic account of cause and effect (Luke 13:1-5). But just as blindness, deafness, paralysis, madness and leprosy were evidence of a deep wrong affecting the nature of things, Jesus' healing touch was evidence of the action of God in bringing in a new order effectively defeating that evil. Nowhere was this more evident than in Jesus' power to restore to life. Whatever we make of the accounts of the raising of the widow of Nain's son (Luke 7:11-17), of the synagogue leader's daughter (Luke 8:40-56) and of Jesus' friend Lazarus (John 11:1-44), they are all recorded in order to elicit belief in the one who said, 'I am the resurrection and the life' (John 11:25). St Paul believed that death was the final enemy, and that death would be destroyed by Christ (1 Corinthians 15:26). Having himself been raised from the dead, death had no more power over Jesus (Romans 6:9).

Jesus' deeds of power that involved healing are not beyond our understanding, although in our desire to explain them we can miss the point of why they were recorded. The stories of his raising people from death are obviously more difficult to explain, and there is a temptation either to dismiss them as legend or to give them some other explanation, such as the person being in a coma or a catatonic state. On the other hand, their theological meaning is more obviously understood.

This may also be true of those other powerful deeds which we describe as nature miracles, in particular those that involved Jesus in acts of rescue or saving. During the storm on the lake he calmed the winds and the waves by command, but he may well have raised his hand as he did so (Matthew 8:26). On the occasion when he appeared to his disciples as they sailed across Lake Galilee, the impetuous Peter jumped into the sea to go and greet Jesus and then got into difficulties and feared for his life. For a while he shared in his master's ability to walk on water, but when he saw how high the waves were he lost heart and began to drown. Jesus immediately reached out his hand and caught him, saying to him, 'You of little faith, why did you doubt?' (Matthew 14:31). Again, it is the meaning of these actions rather than the events themselves that are important, although the reader is, of course, free to accept them as they stand or to find an explanation, such as the possibility that they were actually close to shore and were walking on hidden rocks. But for the Gospel writers they were further examples of Jesus' powerful deeds – his power or authority over nature itself (which was a divine attribute) and the power to save his followers from danger, even when that arose from a failure of trust. For the early Church facing persecution and anxious for its very existence, such accounts would have been important in supporting their faith and encouraging their perseverance.

In his willingness to touch lepers, Jesus showed that he could move beyond the norms of accepted behaviour in order to demonstrate the inclusive nature of his love and therefore that of the kingdom. He showed this same inclusive attitude in his dealings with women and with foreigners – note especially his attitude to the Samaritan woman at the well. The amazement of his followers and others arose both from the fact that he was talking to a woman and from the fact that she was a Samaritan. As John records, 'Jews do not share things in common with Samaritans' (John 4:9) – and certainly not drinking vessels.

The account of Jesus' meeting with the woman at the well points to an important fact in his ministry that is sometimes neglected, namely that he received as well as gave. St Paul reports that Jesus said, 'It is more blessed to give than to receive' (Acts 20:35), although there is no record of Jesus having said this in the Gospels. Nevertheless, it reflects his own example of service, of so often meeting the needs of those who sought his help. At a time when the disciples were disputing who was the most important among them, Jesus reminded them that although he was their leader he was among them as one who serves (Luke 22:27). He was one who gave service rather than looked to others to serve him. This humble giving, highlighted in the giving of his life, has sometimes led Christians to think that they are called only to give and that there is something slightly wrong, or less than perfect, about receiving. But this is a distortion of both what Jesus meant and what he did. He was certainly open-handed in his generosity of welcome and giving. But he knew also how to receive from the hands of others. He depended upon women among his followers to help provide for him; he happily received hospitality from both the respectable and the less than respectable; he received a drink of water from the Samaritan woman; he was given a hand carrying his cross; his tomb was a gift from a friend. There is a blessing that comes through gracious receiving as well as the blessing of giving generously.

- Do you find it more difficult to give graciously or to receive graciously?
- Does it depend on who is giving and who is being given to?

We have seen that Jesus' attitude to women and to outsiders was radical in its openness. His attitude to children might also be seen as distinctive. The disciples were not being cruel when they told the people off who brought their children to Jesus to touch. They may well have been simply protecting him from yet more demands. But the sternness of the disciples' rebuke followed by Jesus' own reaction of indignation seems to indicate that something more fundamental was at stake (Mark 10:13-16). There may have been an issue of status, reflecting the discussion in Mark 9:33-7 where the disciples had argued about who was the greatest and Jesus had taken a child and set it among them saying, 'Whoever welcomes one such child in my name welcomes me.'

The disciples would have assumed that the parents wanting their children to be touched by Jesus were actually asking for them to receive a blessing. It is possible that the disciples objected to this on the grounds that this was an exclusive privilege they alone should have. Such an attitude aroused Jesus' indignation. The children had no claim on him, no rights through which to receive a blessing. They were merely there with nothing to offer but the simple act of receiving what Jesus could bestow on them. The kingdom that Jesus was inviting people to enter was an inclusive one where the only requirement for entry was acceptance of the invitation. There is no deserving, there is no right of privilege, there is no question of earning entry, no required status: children and the poor know this, and that is why the kingdom of heaven is theirs (Matthew 5:3).

This account of Jesus taking the children into his arms and blessing them reflects what Jesus understood about the kingdom being open to all and bringing benefit (blessing) to all who responded to the invitation to enter. In the early Church, and certainly in later centuries, this story was used to support those who argued for the baptism of children. It became a baptismal reading and may also have been used to oppose church leaders who sought to restrict the presence of children in worship or church affairs.

In this story Jesus touched the children and blessed them. Elsewhere the act of blessing was indicated by the raising of the hands without touching. In Luke's account of Jesus' departure from his disciples at the end of the resurrection appearances, Jesus takes his disciples out to the familiar village of Bethany and, 'lifting up his hands, he blessed them. While he was blessing them, he withdrew from them and was carried up into heaven' (Luke 24:50-1). It is common still for clergy to raise a hand during the giving of the blessing at the end of a service.

We have seen that the hand is an instrument of powerful action, of compassionate healing, of saving and welcome and blessing. It is also a symbol of ownership and possession. In chapter 10 of John's Gospel, a number of sayings are brought together that centre on the image of Jesus as the shepherd or gate of the sheepfold. This image has a long tradition, stretching back to the Old Testament (see the previous chapter) where the relationship between the people and their leader or the people and God was described in terms of sheep and shepherd. As has often been noted, by the time of Jesus shepherds had acquired something of a bad reputation, especially those who were hireling shepherds and not the actual owners of the sheep. In using the image of the shepherd, therefore, Jesus goes out of his way to describe himself as a 'good' shepherd – a shepherd who knows his sheep by name, who cares for them and protects them. He is also a powerful shepherd in that he claims that no one will be able to snatch his sheep – an important gift from God – out of his hand (John 10:28-9). Neither can the sheep be snatched from the Father's hand: 'The Father and I are one,' he says (John 10:30). Having something 'in the hand' denotes here not only possession (the sheep belong to the good shepherd) but also the responsibility to keep them safe and protect them. As with the case of Peter's rescue from the waves, this account of a saying by Jesus would have given the early Church courage in the face of danger and persecution. Whatever happened to the 'flock', the followers of Jesus, they could not be snatched from his loving care, nor from being part of his people, the new Israel, the redeemed.

As the time of his Passion drew closer, it is recorded by John that Jesus became aware that not only had the 'sheep' been given to him by the Father as a responsibility and a gift, but that 'all things' had been given into his hands, that he had come from God and that he was going to God (John 13:3). What was in fact in his hands was the knowledge that in coming from God he had followed the path of humility, and that in going to God he would have to follow the path of humiliation. If in doing this it was understood that he was doing so as God, then the omnipotence of this God is expressed in being humble to the point of impotence. Immediately after this saying of Jesus, John reports him stripping off his outer robe, tying a towel around his waist and proceeding to perform the action of the lowest servant – washing his disciples' feet. In Jesus, status, possession and responsibility are all conveyed through service.

As the evening proceeded Jesus would take bread in his hands, bless it and break it. He would take the cup of wine, bless it and share it. There may have been something distinctive about the way he always did this, so distinctive that when he did it later at the home of the two companions whom he had joined on the road to Emmaus, it convinced them that he was alive again (Luke 24:30-5). But on the night of the Last Supper, this action of taking bread and wine, of breaking and sharing, became deeply significant and symbolic for what would happen the next day when his body was broken on the cross and his blood spilt. It was to become the central act of remembrance and of communion in the liturgy of the Church as, together, his followers would see bread and wine taken in the hands of the priest, the bread broken and the wine shared as Jesus had done. It is as though we are being told that this matter was in Jesus' hands: having his body broken and his blood spilt was in his hands, no matter by whose hands it was actually done on Good Friday.

> • How do you understand the saying, 'This is my body; this is my blood'?

Yet if all things were, in fact, in Jesus' hands, there is a sense that he handed them and himself over to others. The trigger action, the tipping point, was seen to be the act of betrayal by Judas. 'See, the hour is at hand, and the Son of Man is betrayed into the hands of sinners' (Matthew 26:45). In his book *The Stature of Waiting*, W. H. Vanstone argues that the word for 'betrayal' should more correctly be translated 'handing over'.[7] It wasn't simply that Judas handed Jesus over to the authorities; it was that Jesus handed himself over to others – indeed, that God handed himself over to men and women. God put himself into

---

7. W. H. Vanstone, *The Stature of Waiting* (Darton, Longman & Todd, 1982).

our hands. Jesus put himself into the hands of those who would now arrest him, try him, convict him and crucify him. To this extent he was agent rather than victim. The Passion was what he was doing rather than what was being done to him. It was the working out of his risking putting all things, which were his by right, into the hands of others and, most significantly, putting himself into their hands, and doing so for love's sake. This wasn't martyrdom; it was the sacrificial cost of love.

Those hands that had healed, blessed, saved, protected, broken bread, shared wine, and finally handed over, were now nailed to a crosspiece, pinning Jesus down. The likelihood is that the nails actually went through his wrists rather than through the palms of his hands, but it is his hands that are traditionally mentioned and which in pictures of the crucifixion are seen to be nailed. It was his hands that bore the recognisable wounds of crucifixion and which he showed to his disciples after his resurrection. For Thomas they were the proof he needed before he could believe that Jesus was no longer dead. 'Unless I see the mark of the nails in his hands, and put my finger in the mark of the nails and my hand in his side, I will not believe' (John 20:25). The wounded hands and side were a way of knowing that this person who appeared so mysteriously to the disciples as they huddled together in fear on that first Easter evening was none other than their Lord who had died so ignominiously the previous Friday. In an experience that was such a mixture of what was known and what was novel, it was the wounded hands that provided evidence of continuity. The very physicality of those hands was part of the experience of resurrection, and the account of them is part of the justification for the belief that it was a bodily resurrection.

c. Feet

It was noted earlier that part of the debate about the central figure in the Ghent altar piece revolves around the fact that while some aspects of the portrayal indicate that this is God the Father, other aspects indicate that it is intended to be Christ, the Son. The figure's feet are shod, leading, in this instance, to the conclusion that this is God the Father. In the religious art of that time it was normal for Jesus to be depicted without shoes or sandals on his feet. It was a sign of his humility.

In Arab and Middle Eastern culture, hitting someone with a shoe or throwing a shoe at someone is considered to be a deep insult. President Bush experienced this in 2008 when a shoe was thrown at him during a press conference at the US embassy. There was a similar incident in Egypt in 2013 during the visit of President Ahmadinejad. When Saddam Hussein's statue was toppled in Baghdad in April 2003, Iraqis swarmed around it, striking it with their shoes. Professor Faegheh Shirazi of the University of Texas stated in an interview, 'Throwing a shoe or hitting someone with a shoe or showing the bottom of your shoe when sitting with legs up on a chair and facing another person all are culturally unacceptable and are considered to be a grave insult and belittling to a person.'[8] When John the Baptist said that he was not worthy even to undo the thongs of Jesus' sandals (Mark 1:7), he was indicating just how much more important Jesus was than himself. The shoe is considered dirty because it is on the ground and associated with the foot, the lowest part of the body.

The Urban Dictionary notes that the phrase 'Jesus feet' means messy, nasty, cut, bleeding or crusty feet, derived from the understanding that Jesus walked everywhere in dusty, stony

---

8. Alan Duke, 'Why shoe throwing is "incredibly offensive" ', CNN, 7 February 2013. Available at edition.cnn.com/2013/02/06/world/meast/shoe-throwing-significance (accessed 15 January 2015).

conditions. 'Anyone with nasty, messed up feet can be said to have Jesus Feet'.[9]

In the Middle East, feet have always been regarded as unclean. When guests reclined for a meal they would tuck their feet behind them so as not to insult other guests by pointing their feet at them. It was the lowliest servants who had the task of washing the feet of guests or of their master. When Jesus, as host at the last meal with his disciples, wanted to demonstrate the nature of the service he expected of his followers, he set them an example by washing their feet (John 13:1-11). Normal etiquette would be for a host to offer guests water to wash their feet after a journey, or to command a servant to wash them. A host who failed to do so was not merely neglecting a common courtesy; it was close to being an insult.

These factors provide something of the cultural background to the story of the woman who washed Jesus' feet with her tears, wiping them with her hair and anointing them with perfume. Her actions were outrageous in polite society and would themselves have marked her out as an immoral woman quite apart from her reputation as a sinner (prostitute). The story appears in the Gospels in various versions (Matthew 26:1-13; Mark 14:1-9; Luke 7:36-50; John 12:1-11).[10]

The host, a Pharisee, had performed none of the courtesies expected of a host – he had not greeted Jesus with a kiss either on the cheek or on the hand, and he had not provided water for his feet to be washed. By contrast, the woman showed immense gratitude, devotion and humility by washing and kissing his feet. The host had not shown his respect for his guest by offering the refreshment of pouring olive oil on his head. By contrast, the woman anointed his feet with perfumed

9. Urban Dictionary. Available at http://www.urbandictionary.com/define.php?term=Jesus+Feet (accessed 2 January 2015).
10. For a fuller commentary on these accounts see John Cox, *The Week That Changed the World.* (Kevin Mayhew, 2012) pp.43–53.

ointment. Olive oil was relatively cheap, but even that would not be wasted on a person's feet – let alone the very expensive ointment the woman used. The accounts of this incident are rich in symbolism and various theological meaning, but at their simplest they indicate the contrast of attitude between the sinful but adoring woman and the self-righteous but neglectful Pharisee. The contrast is heightened in the accounts that have the woman anointing Jesus' feet rather than his head.

A woman is also involved in another incident that would have been regarded as unusual, if not shocking, in the culture of the time. We are told that Jesus spent some time with his friends Mary, Martha and Lazarus at their home in Bethany. He obviously had something of a special relationship with the trio. In Luke's Gospel we are told of a particular incident in which Mary listened to Jesus while her sister Martha scurried around sorting out the domestic chores. Martha's complaint and Jesus' response that Mary had chosen 'the better part' (Luke 10:42) have given rise to a contrasting understanding of discipleship: active service and quiet, reflective attention. For our purposes, the significance of the story rests with Mary. Martha welcomed Jesus but her sister Mary 'sat at the Lord's feet and listened to what he was saying' (Luke 10:39).

> • What do you think society and the church has still to learn about the place of women?

Learning from a master is often described as 'sitting at his feet'. This is was what Mary was doing literally, but in doing so she was also taking up the position of a student with a rabbi. The term 'rabbi' was used informally for any teacher and indicated the disciples' respect for the 'master' (which underlies the meaning of the word 'rabbi'). It only became a formal title, recognised by a form of 'ordination', after the destruction of the Temple in AD 70. Nevertheless, as David Bivin has said:

> The designation 'rabbi' may still be more helpful than any other in conveying a correct image of Jesus to the average Christian reader. If this designation suggests that Jesus was recognized as a teacher in his day and that he was famous enough to draw students to himself, then 'rabbi,' although anachronistic, perhaps serves a useful purpose.[11]

The Gospel writers certainly record Jesus being addressed as 'Rabbi' and go out of their way to contrast the teaching of the 'rabbis' to that of Jesus. It is therefore not impossible that Luke was indicating that Mary was indeed acting as a student with her rabbi. If that was indeed the case, it reveals again Jesus' willingness for situations to arise that broke the social norm. While it was not unknown for women to join groups of men as they listened to the teachings of a rabbi, it was not acceptable for a woman to do so on her own, which is the situation implied here.

Sitting at the feet of someone thus indicated the relationship of student to teacher. Falling or kneeling at the feet of someone indicated the relationship of humble service to a master, or adoration to a religious figure. On a number of occasions the Gospels record people falling at Jesus' feet. Among the more unexpected is the case of Jairus (Mark 5:21-3). He was a man of repute, a respected leader at a synagogue, and for him to throw himself at Jesus' feet was a highly undignified thing to have done. It was a show of humility, and by implication was in stark contrast to the attitude of so many of the religious leaders in their contact with Jesus.

---

11. David Bivin, 'Was Jesus a Rabbi?' Available at www.jerusalemperspective.com/2182 (June 1988; revised December 2012) (accessed 2nd January 2015).

At the start of a section of Mark's Gospel which some scholars have described as 'The Gentile Mission', Mark tells the story of the Syrophoenician woman, a woman who was not Jewish either by descent or by religious conviction (Mark 7:24-30). She threw herself at Jesus' feet, no doubt out of her desperate desire for Jesus to heal her young daughter, who was possessed by a demon. But her action could also be interpreted as one of worship – the worship offered by a Gentile, just as the Gentile Magi had knelt in homage to Jesus at his birth (Matthew 2:11), foreshadowing the conversion of Gentiles as the mission of the early Church spread beyond Palestine. Jesus' reaction to the woman was initially comparatively hostile as he reminded her that the needs of the children (of Israel) were to be met before those of the dogs (the Gentiles). The woman appeared to take no offence at this and indeed seemed to accept that this was the right order of things. But her persistence also speaks of her belief that the Gentiles as well as the Jews were to be healed and saved by Jesus, and he granted her request. She went home and found her daughter healed. Among the early Church this form of the story may have given weight to the argument that the Gentiles would be saved along with the Jews and would not, as others believed, have to wait until the end of the age.

The demoniac, too, fell at Jesus' feet and showed obeisance before him (Luke 8:28), indicating that even the demons recognised Jesus for who he was. The people of the area were surprised to find the man in his right mind and clothed, sitting at Jesus feet. The one who had worshipped even when possessed now sat as a student at the feet of the teacher. Later he begged Jesus to allow him to become a disciple, but Jesus instead 'commissioned' him as an evangelist, 'saying, "Return to your home, and declare how much God has done for you."

So he went away, proclaiming throughout the city how much Jesus had done for him' (Luke 8:38, 39).

We saw in the previous section that the wounded hands of Jesus were part of the evidence for the fact that Jesus had risen from the dead, that his was a bodily resurrection and not merely a spiritual event. Luke tells us that Jesus showed the frightened disciples both his hands and his feet to help them believe it was indeed him and not a ghost (Luke 24:36-40). This and the fact that he asked for some broiled fish and ate it in their presence reinforced not only his identity but its physicality – a continuation of his bodily self in spite of the changes that resurrection also involved. This was the one who greeted the women in the garden that first Easter morning and whose feet they had held as they worshipped him (Matthew 28:9).

> • What are appropriate gestures and actions these days to demonstrate the honour we give to the one we worship?

d. Roles and titles

It is noteworthy that of the seven 'I am' sayings of Jesus recorded in John's Gospel, only one relates to a human image – the good shepherd (John 10:11). Of the others, some have direct reference to an object, such as the true vine (John 15:1), the gate of the sheepfold (John 10:9) or bread (John 6:35). The remainder have a more abstract reference: the way, the truth and the life (John 14:6); light of the world (John 8:12); the resurrection and the life (John 11:25). Each of these sayings and images is rich in theological significance.

The vine was an image used in the Old Testament for Israel. God was said to have 'planted' this vine: 'You brought a vine out of Egypt; you drove out the nations and planted it' (Psalm 80:8). He looked for it to produce a fine crop of grapes and too often he was disappointed (Jeremiah 8:13). The powerful and telling parable of the vineyard in Isaiah 5 begins, 'Let me sing for my beloved my love-song concerning his vineyard;' and concludes at verse 7 with this damning statement:

The vineyard of the Lord of hosts
is the house of Israel,
and the people of Judah are his pleasant planting;
he expected justice,
but saw bloodshed;
righteousness,
but heard a cry!

The vine was therefore a corporate image indicating the whole nation, and Israel had been found to be fruitless. There is some evidence – such as in Matthew 19:28; 20:21; Luke 22:30 – that the early Christian tradition saw the followers of Jesus as constituting the new Israel with the disciples taking top places. Jesus, however, does not include them in his saying about the true vine. He takes this community image and uses it about himself – he is the new, true Israel, and it is only as others are 'in him' that the new people of God will be created.

The foundation of the life of the new Israel was its renewed relationship with God, made possible in and through Jesus, the Christ. Jesus is seen as the way to the Father, the means of entry into that new relationship. More than that, he is the unique, only **Way**: 'No one comes to the Father except through me' (John 14.6).

In the image of the **gate of the sheepfold**, Jesus conveys the notion that he is the legitimate, safe way to the father. John 10 makes extended use of imagery from the pastoral life of sheep and shepherds. Two situations are envisaged: the first is the care of sheep brought off the hills and collected together in the village where the large communal sheepfold was secured by a stout gate guarded by a watchman. The second is the situation out on the hills where each shepherd looked after his own sheep and at night would take them to a small stone pen where there was no gate but just a gap in the sheepfold wall. The shepherd would lie across the entrance to keep the sheep secure. Jesus is thinking of this when he says, 'I am the gate for the sheep' (John 10:7). The thieves and bandits he goes on to mention are not the prophets who went before him but those who made false promises to the people about a wonderful future, usually on the back of war and spilt blood. They were dangerous 'charlatans' in the business of providing a way to God and his promised kingdom. Jesus may have had the Zealots in mind: the way they promised was the way of violence. By contrast, those who enter through Jesus will be saved and able to come and go to find pasture. The phrase 'come and go' was commonly used in Hebrew to mean a life that was safe and secure.

Out on the hills, life was hard and at times dangerous. The owner–shepherd had full responsibility for his sheep and they were dependent upon him to keep them safe and to care for them. Some owners used hired men to act as shepherds. They could not always be relied on, especially if danger threatened, either from wild animals or thieves. Rather than risk their lives they would often simply run. They gave shepherds a bad reputation.

Jesus, by contrast, described himself as the good shepherd, a shepherd who knew his sheep and whose sheep knew him (John 10:14). There was trust and recognition, and at its heart was the fact that **the good shepherd** would be willing to lay down his life for the sheep, not because he was forced to but out of his care for the sheep: 'No one takes [my life] from me, but I lay it down of my own accord . . . and I have power to take it up again' (John 10:18). In this image of the good shepherd, Jesus was drawing upon its usage in the Old Testament for a leader of Israel and for God (see chapter 1 section g) as well as relating his teaching to the lives and common experience of the people. The reference to his death was an indication that his way – the way to God – was not to be found in force of arms as the Zealots believed, but in the self-sacrifice of love. Life was to be found through death – that resurrection life that is promised now and stretches into eternity.

- What modern alternative might be used for the image of the good shepherd, especially in an urban setting?

Such life is, of course, much more than physical existence – it is that fullness of life, the life of the spirit that Jesus said he was bringing to people. Such life could only be sustained by the one who made it possible – Jesus himself. It was in this sense that he claimed to be the bread of life (John 6:35), the bread that satisfies all that the human spirit longs for, all that it hungers after. To 'partake' of Jesus is, of course, a continuation of the image, and in that sense it is not to be understood literally, even when Jesus went on to say that the bread is in fact his flesh.

It is generally agreed that John is conveying eucharistic theology here. Unlike the other Gospel writers, John does not record the institution of the Lord's Supper. There is no account of breaking bread and sharing wine on the night before the crucifixion. John, as it were, disperses this event throughout the Gospel by allusion and thematic reference. At Cana, Jesus turned water into wine (John 2:1-11). At the feeding of the 5000 he took bread, gave thanks and distributed the bread to those present (John 6:11). In the saying about the vine, some people see allusion to the wine of the Eucharist. And here Jesus spoke of his flesh being bread that his followers feed on; his blood is what they drink so that they may enjoy eternal life. His flesh and blood are the bread and the wine that sustain the spirit of the individual, and they also sustain the life of the Church, the Body (see below).

With language like this, it is not totally surprising that Christians were mistakenly accused of being cannibals! While the incumbent of a London parish, I was approached by a member of the congregation about being received into the Church of England. The man had been brought up a Catholic but in his middle years he had become a regular worshipper at my church. He never received communion. When I asked him why, he said that he just could not get his head round the thought that he would be eating Jesus' flesh. His understanding reflected the way he had been taught as a child. We discussed different ways in which communion might be understood, and sometime later he asked to be received into the Church and became a regular communicant.

e. Son

Son of Mary

While there are numerous myths of gods mating with human partners, there is something that is both awesome and shocking in the claim that a teenage girl from Nazareth conceived a child 'of the Holy Spirit', the Spirit of the God of the Hebrews. The Jewish faith had been so fierce in its opposition to any suggestion that its God was like the gods of the nations around, with their cultic prostitutes and their notions of divine sexual involvement. Yet here, according to two of the Gospels, was the presence of the Divine on the historical scene in a very specific way through the physical agency of a young woman, a virgin. Whatever we conclude about the sensitive question of the historicity of the Virgin birth, it has to be recognised that Matthew and Luke, by including it in their Gospels, were taking a big risk. Plenty of people would have concluded that here was just another folk myth doing the rounds.

In Matthew we have the account of how Joseph was made aware that his fiancée Mary was to have a child 'from the Holy Spirit' (Matthew 1:20), while Luke records that Mary herself was told that she would become pregnant as the power of the Most High would 'overshadow' her (Luke 1:35). While this is not the place to go into detail, it is enough to note that the differences between the Matthean and Lucan birth narratives are sufficient for most scholars to conclude that neither knew of the other nor had a straightforward common source. There are events around the birth which are quite different in the two accounts, such as Matthew's visit of the wise men and Luke's visit of the shepherds. Matthew makes use of the Isaiah prophecy, 'Look the virgin shall conceive and bear a son, and they shall name him Emmanuel' (Matthew 1:23), while Luke offers no such textual reference but nevertheless emphasises more than Matthew does the fact that Mary was a virgin. We can note that the Isaiah verse was not in fact used in contemporary Jewish circles as a prediction of the birth of the Messiah by a virgin since the word simply referred to a young woman. Matthew used the text for his own purposes and built his account around it.

Even where the accounts have features in common, they are presented in widely different ways. In Matthew the focus is on Joseph, and Mary plays a somewhat passive role. In Luke, Mary is much more central but, importantly, the story is 'twinned' with that of Elizabeth and the birth of John the Baptist.

The Christian tradition has, from quite early times through its liturgies and credal formulae, expressed belief in the Virgin birth (or more strictly the Virgin conception). In terms of the New Testament record, this is in some ways surprising. Not only do two of the Gospels make no mention of Jesus' birth; they do not seem in the slightest embarrassed by its absence. Mark is self-confidently assured in his belief that the gospel of Jesus Christ can be told with all that is necessary for salvation by beginning with Jesus' appearance as a man. John has no birth narratives either, and although his prologue sets the account of Jesus in the wide time frame of 'in the beginning' and of the pre-existent Word, he too tells of Jesus' first appearing on the scene as a fully grown man. Neither Matthew nor Luke, having given their accounts, refer to the matter of the Virgin birth again, and there is no direct reference to it anywhere else in the New Testament. It does not appear to have been part of the earliest Christian message.

Such considerations as these, and many others, have given rise to questions about the historicity of the Virgin birth as a physical, biological event, and to a scepticism readily jumped upon by those wishing to discredit the Christian faith as a whole. Scholars vary widely in their understanding of what is in fact being presented in the birth/infancy narratives, from those who accept it as historical fact to those who see it akin to legend, such as would attach itself to famous heroes. It is now virtually impossible to get behind the accounts to know with any certainty what the historical events might have been. This is not to deny there may have been some, but merely to suggest caution in making claims that are not supportable by the evidence available. One thing that can be said with certainty, however, is that belief in the Virgin birth came to be sufficiently widely and firmly embedded in the Church so that it took root in the later creeds: 'conceived by the Holy Spirit, born of the virgin Mary'.

One way of exploring this issue without resorting either to simple history or to legend is to see the story as a theological reflection in narrative form of what came to be believed about Jesus after his death and resurrection. The Gospel writers' concern is not biographical as we understand it, but theological. Accounts of the Virgin birth emerged in certain circles of the early Church where interest was shown in the birth and origins of Jesus, but it was not apparently known in those communities associated with Mark, John or Paul.

Describing Jesus as the son of Mary draws undeniable attention to his humanity. Jesus' human origins are there in the very physical world of womb and placenta, of labour and birth. The record of his birth leaves us in no doubt about this commonality with all humanity. He did not appear from nowhere on the banks of the Jordan as a man of 30 ready formed. He experienced what all of us have gone through in birth and infancy, childhood and the teenage years. He had to grow and mature; he did not emerge like the legendary Athene did – fully formed from the head of Zeus. Luke says that he was obedient to his parents and 'increased in wisdom and in years, and in divine and human favour' (Luke 2:52). His full identification with humankind, so important theologically if he were to be the saviour of all, was not an abstraction but a physical reality.

So there is some element of contradiction. Jesus was human like the rest of us and yet his origin indicates that he was different. There were plenty of legends that heightened the reputation of heroes by suggesting abnormal births, and giving prominence to the fact that Mary was a virgin who conceived through the power of the Holy Spirit could have simply encouraged the view that here too was a legend. Alongside this was the concept that human sinfulness was 'transmitted' through the act of sexual intercourse so that we 'inherit' our sinful nature from our parents. All of us are caught up in this. Yet the belief developed that Jesus, as a perfect, 'sinless' human being, must have in some way avoided this. That he was born of a virgin gave an explanation while at the same time setting him to this extent apart from the common human experience.

More importantly, and certainly more anciently, the Virgin birth account offered a way to convey very directly the fundamental belief that the coming of Jesus (the Saviour) who was Emmanuel (God with us) was unquestionably the result of the purpose, initiative and activity of God. It was not the work of human beings but of God. It was God's enormous and generous gift. Luke, for his part, understood the whole story of Jesus – his life, death and resurrection, and the emergence and spread of the mission of the Church – as directed and enabled by God's Spirit. So the Holy Spirit had to be there at the beginning. Mary's part was that of humanity placing itself at the service of God so that God's purposes could be achieved: 'Here am I, the servant of the Lord; let it be with me according to your word' (Luke 1:38).

- What would you feel had been lost to your understanding of Jesus if there were not the accounts of the 'virgin birth'?

Son of David

Matthew's intention seems to have been different. He certainly
didn't deny that Jesus came as the agent of God on God's
initiative but, as we have already noted, there were two distinct
elements in the way he set out his account: the reference to
scriptural prophecy and the role of Joseph.

From the outset, Matthew was concerned to show that Jesus
emerged as the fulfilment of the highest hopes and expectations
of the Jewish people as expressed in their Scriptures through
their prophets. Writing for Christian communities whose
origins were Jewish, he needed to show that Jesus was not some
heretical upstart but was the Messiah promised to the people of
Israel. He did so by drawing upon the Hebrew Scriptures and
showing how Jesus fulfilled them. In the birth and infancy
accounts he quotes:

> Look, the virgin shall conceive and bear a son, and they
> shall name him Emmanuel.
>
> *Matthew 1:23, quoting Isaiah 7:14*

> And you Bethlehem, in the land of Judah,
> are by no means the least among the rulers of Judah;
> for from you shall come a ruler
> who is to shepherd my people Israel.
>
> *Matthew 2:6, quoting Micah 5:2*

> Out of Egypt have I called my son.
>
> *Matthew 2:15, quoting Hosea 11:1*

> A voice was heard in Ramah,
> wailing and loud lamentation,

Rachel weeping for her children;
she refused to be consoled, because they are no more.

Matthew 2:18, quoting Jeremiah 35:15

In Matthew's account, the angel came not to Mary, but to Joseph. His message was one of reassurance to explain to Joseph what had happened to the girl he was engaged to and to give an explanation that, while mysterious, was not shameful. Joseph was, significantly, addressed as 'son of David' (Matthew 1:20). This linked Jesus into the line of King David and reinforced the genealogy provided by Matthew as the opening of his Gospel (Matthew 1:1-16). Luke made a similar point in the genealogy that appears in chapter 3 of his Gospel, and also through the account of the census which required Joseph to go to his ancestral town – Bethlehem, the town of David (Luke 2:4). Scholars generally agree that the two genealogies are not historically accurate, though they are theologically significant.

John's Gospel records a wrangle among the crowd concerning just who Jesus was. Some said he was the Messiah, but this was countered with the argument that the Messiah could not come from Galilee but, being descended from King David, would have to come from David's home town of Bethlehem. 'So there was a division in the crowd because of him' (John 7:40-7). For the Gospel reader this would have simply reinforced the belief that Jesus was both Messiah and a descendant of David.

The Gospels do record, however, a couple of events when Jesus was directly addressed as 'Son of David.' As Jesus left (approached) the busy town of Jericho, a blind beggar, possibly called Bartimaeus and possibly there were two of them, called out to catch his attention, 'Jesus, Son of David, have mercy on me' (Matthew 20:29-34; Mark 10:46-52; Luke 18:35-43). The title is not used again in the Gospels and may simply have been spoken out of respect.

On Jesus' entry into Jerusalem, Matthew reports the crowd proclaiming, 'Hosanna to the Son of David! Blessed is he who comes in the name of the Lord!' (Matthew 21:9, 15). The other Gospel writers record the event but omit any direct reference to the Son of David. The quotation used in the crowd's proclamation comes from Psalm 118:26: 'Blessed is the one who comes in the name of the Lord,' and again that has no direct reference to David. Mark refers to the coming kingdom of David: 'Hosanna! Blessed is the one who comes in the name of the Lord! Blessed is the coming kingdom of our ancestor David! (Mark 11:9, 10), while Luke has, 'Blessed is the king who comes in the name of the Lord! (Luke 19:38). It appears to be clear that some such proclamation was made and that it had royal associations. It is doubtful, however, that Matthew was right in thinking that Jesus was directly addressed here as Son of David. Geza Vermes has pointed out that the words translated as 'Hosanna to the son of David' would have actually been meaningless in Aramaic.[12]

While it is therefore questionable that the title 'Son of David' was widely used for Jesus in his lifetime, it was useful in supporting the belief that Jesus was the Messiah.

Son of Man

Of all the titles associated with Jesus, none has caused as much controversy as 'Son of Man'. There are almost as many opinions about it as there are scholars and books on the subject. As a title it occurs frequently in the Gospels, only once in Acts and twice in Revelation. In the most explicitly theological sections of the New Testament – the Epistles – where one would expect it to appear most often if it were a recognised Christological title, it does not appear at all. In the synoptic Gospels the phrase is

---

12. Geza Vermes, *Jesus the Jew* (SCM Press, 1983), p.157.

only used by Jesus and is never used as a way of addressing Jesus. While scholars today discuss and argue about the title, its use in Jesus' time aroused no contemporary questions or objection, which may well indicate that it had no specific significance for faith about Jesus.

An incident in John's Gospel, although not without problems, begins to suggest one way of understanding what was going on. John reports Jesus as saying:

> 'And I, when am lifted up from the earth, will draw all people to myself.' He said this to indicate the kind of death he was to die. The crowd answered him, 'We have heard from the law that the Messiah remains for ever. How can you say that the Son of Man must be lifted up? Who is this Son of Man?'

> *John 12:32-4*

The crucial aspect of the crowd's question is not about the title 'Son of Man' but about the nature of the death the Son of Man would endure. To be 'lifted up' was not a reference to Jesus' ascension but to his death by crucifixion. The way the crowd expressed its question indicates that Jesus had actually said that it was 'the Son of Man' who would be lifted up. 'Son of Man' therefore equates to 'I' and appears to have been a way Jesus frequently referred to himself. There was nothing particularly strange about this, and parallels have occasionally been found in non-biblical Aramaic writings. The phrase was used as a circumlocution for the self out of modesty, or in contexts where death or humiliation are mentioned.

In Daniel 7, use is made of the phrase 'like a son of man' ('like a human being', NRSV) to describe a figure Daniel saw in one of his night visions (dreams). In the explanation of the dream given by 'one of the attendants', it is clear that this figure stood for 'the holy ones of the Most High,' who would 'receive the kingdom and possess the kingdom for ever – for ever and ever' (Daniel 7:18). The figure is therefore not an individual but a collective title. Some scholars suggest that this means it could not have been used of Jesus as an individual. On the other hand, it is also argued that just as Jesus was seen in some sense as the embodiment of the new Israel, so too he was the embodiment of humankind, the representative man, the new Adam, as Paul would have put it.

So the discussion continues as to whether Son of Man was anything more than just a way Jesus referred to himself. Some argue that the phrase was so much in common use as a circumlocution that it could never become a title of Christological significance. Others remain convinced that it was indeed used as a title by Jesus with Messianic and eschatological significance.

Son of God – Messiah

While we have seen that Jesus was never addressed as 'Son of Man', he was often described in the New Testament as 'Son of God'. Christians these days would naturally assume that this was the title that most obviously declared his divinity. It certainly became that, and was codified in credal statements, such as in the Nicene Creed:

> We believe in one Lord, Jesus Christ,
> the only Son of God,
> eternally begotten of the Father,
> God from God, Light from Light,
> true God from true God,
> begotten, not made,
> of one Being with the Father.

But if we seek to understand what the title would have meant among the earliest Christians, it is important to remember that

a) the Nicene Creed is the product of a very non-Jewish way of thinking, and b) it wasn't formulated until the fourth century. In considering the meaning it had in Jesus' time, it will be important to look at who addressed Jesus by such a title and in what sense Jesus used it of himself.

Perhaps unexpectedly, we begin with the occasions when it is recorded that it was demons who addressed Jesus as 'Son of God'. 'Whenever the unclean spirits saw him, they fell down before him and shouted, "You are the Son of God!"' (Mark 3:11). The violent man was possessed by a legion of unclean spirits and lived among the tombs in the country of the Gerasenes. He spotted Jesus from a distance, ran and bowed down before him and shouted at the top of his voice: 'What have you to do with me, Jesus, Son of the Most High God?' (Mark 5:7; see also Luke 8:28; Matthew 8:29). Among those whom we are told Jesus healed were a number whose sickness was understood at the time in terms of possession by demons or evil spirits. In each case, Jesus healed the person of their sickness, exorcising the demon. It appears therefore that the title was associated with Jesus as a charismatic healer and exorcist and, by extension, as a general miracle worker.

At the beginning of his ministry, immediately after his baptism, the Spirit led Jesus out into the wilderness where, after a period of fasting, he was visited by 'the devil'. In the first temptation the devil said, 'If you are the Son of God, command this stone to become a loaf of bread' (Luke 4:3), and in the third (in Luke's order of the temptations):

> The devil took him to Jerusalem, and placed him on the pinnacle of the temple, saying to him, 'If you are the Son of God, throw yourself down from here, for it is written,
> 'He will command his angels concerning you,
> to protect you',
> and

'On their hands they will bear you up,
so that you will not dash your foot against a stone.'
Jesus answered him, 'It is said "Do not put the Lord your
God to the test." '

Luke 4:9-12

The word translated 'if' could equally mean 'since', so Satan was not necessarily expressing doubt about Jesus' sonship but assuming it. On the one hand it was as a miracle worker that Satan addressed Jesus, tempting him to perform miraculous wonders just to prove that he could. But the meaning of the title can also be understood in the context of its Old Testament usage where it refers to the true Israel which was the servant of God. This lies behind the words heard at Jesus' baptism: 'This is my Son, the Beloved, with whom I am well pleased' (Matthew 3:17), and behind Satan's use of the title for Jesus. Jesus, like the true Israel, was God's servant, his son.

In the Old Testament, 'son of God' is used of angels, of Israel both as a nation and as individuals, and of kings of Israel. Christians have never suggested that Jesus was an angel, and use of the title in relation to Jesus simply in the way it was accorded to any Jew does not indicate the distinctive way it was applied to Jesus by the Gospels. So what about a king? In Psalm 2:7, the Lord says, 'You are my son; today I have begotten you.' He is addressing the king. The prophet Nathan was instructed by the Lord to tell king David, 'I will be a father to him, and he shall be a son to me' (2 Samuel 7:14). The title of 'son of God' later came to be associated not simply with the reigning monarch but with the Davidic ruler of the future, the Messiah. When the followers of Jesus came to believe that he was the Messiah, the title 'son of God' accompanied it.

We can see these two titles brought together at a watershed moment at Caesarea Philippi when Jesus asked his disciples what people were making of him. Who did they say the Son of Man (Jesus) was? The disciples replied that some said he was John the Baptist, Elijah, Jeremiah or one of the prophets. 'He said to them, "But who do you say that I am?" Simon Peter answered, "You are the Messiah, the Son of the living God." ' (Matthew 16:13-16). While in Matthew's Gospel this is followed by Jesus congratulating Peter, in Mark's Gospel Jesus immediately forbade his disciples to tell anyone. When he then told them that he would suffer and be handed over and put to death, Peter showed that his understanding of what the Messiah would do was at complete odds with the way Jesus understood himself, so much so that Jesus addressed Peter as 'Satan!'(Mark 8:27-33). There is dispute among the scholars as to whether or not Jesus accepted the title of 'Son of God', or indeed that of 'Messiah', on this occasion. Peter's confession is centred on Jesus as Messiah, backed up, as it were, by a description of him as a powerful agent of God (Son of God).

For Mark, the main point is in the different views of Peter and Jesus as to what that Messiahship entailed. Jesus' identity as a divinely empowered Messiah was confirmed, and the nature of that Messiahship was gradually revealed as Jesus continued to teach his disciples that as Messiah he must suffer and die.

That Mark firmly believed that Jesus was indeed the Messiah can be seen by the opening of his Gospel: 'The beginning of the good news of Jesus Christ [the Messiah], the Son of God' (Mark 1:1). The additional title 'Son of God' does not appear in some of the manuscripts, which has led some people to believe it was a later addition. But there is no reason to think that Mark, along with the early Church, did not believe Jesus to be the Son of God. That is not the same, however, as saying he believed Jesus to be the second person of the Trinity, as came to be formulated much later and from different, non-Jewish thought forms.

Consideration of the title 'Son of God' has brought us, almost inevitably, to the title of Messiah, the Christ, the Anointed, and with it to how Jesus understood his own identity. In common with contemporary Jewish belief, Jesus believed that Israel's God was bringing in his kingdom, heralding the defeat of evil and the return of Yahweh to Zion. Jesus was distinctive in believing that all this would come about in and through him as the Messiah. This, as N. T. Wright has argued, was the centre of Jesus' sense of vocation. It informed and shaped what he said and what he did.[13]

Although contemporary Jewish understandings of exactly what the Messiah would do form no single coherent programme, the king/messiah figure was central, and key tasks focused on the rebuilding or reforming of the Temple and fighting for Israel to overcome her enemies. It was with such expectations that the crowd greeted Jesus on his entry into Jerusalem. But Jesus' understanding of his role as Messiah was very different. He made no attempt to fulfil the crowd's expectations. When he did go to the Temple his action was a prophetic threat to its very existence and its worship, and he never had any intention of leading an armed rebellion against the Roman authorities. The events at the end of the week would vindicate what he had been saying for a long time, that the Messiah would suffer and be put to death.

Jesus had made no secret of this distinctive understanding of the role, and although the disciples were slow or reluctant to accept Jesus' insistence on the fact that he would suffer and be put to death, nevertheless they still identified Jesus as the Messiah. So while Jesus' interpretation of his role as Messiah was different to that of his contemporaries, there must have been sufficient similarities for there to be a common

13. N. T. Wright, *Jesus and the Victory of God* (SPCK, 1999).

recognition of the role and title. This had built up over the time of his ministry, by word and action. The crowd recognised and declared his royal status at the time of the entry into Jerusalem. He reinforced this by riding to the Temple Mount, which was equivalent to declaring his ownership of the Temple – the Temple being clearly associated in this way with the king in the Old Testament from David to the Maccabeans. His 'cleansing' of the Temple and his pronouncement concerning its worship were further assertions of the Messianic role in terms of bringing Temple reform (destruction) and the fact that the day of God's action had arrived: he drove out the traders and declared the temple to be the place where all nations could pray (Mark 11:15-17; see also Zechariah 14:21).

At Jesus' trial, the high priest asked Jesus if he were the Messiah:

> Again the high priest asked him, 'Are you the Messiah, the Son of the Blessed One?' Jesus said, 'I am; and
> "you will see the Son of Man [me]
> seated at the right hand of the Power",
> and "coming with the clouds of heaven." '

> *Mark 14:61, 62*

The focus of the question is on Messiahship, and 'Son of the Blessed One' is simply the title of the special servant of God. It has nothing to do with Jesus' place in the Trinity, nor does it imply incarnation. Jesus came clean and accepted the Messianic title. His reply has reference to two Messianic texts – Psalm 110 and Daniel 7:13, 14 – and was Jesus' way of saying, 'I will be vindicated in that belief and you will see it for yourself.' It was a daring and radical claim to make, given how little like a Messiah this figure, humiliated, on trial, in danger of his life, would have appeared.

Jesus was executed by the Roman authorities on the grounds of his claim to be the messianic leader of Israel, a charge brought by the Jewish authorities which he had admitted and which was written out on the board above his head on the cross: 'The King of the Jews'. But Jesus' self-understanding appears to have gone beyond even this. He had believed himself called to live and speak out of the conviction that in and through him the God of the Hebrews was returning to Zion as he had promised. And in doing so, Jesus had discovered a relationship with God that could only be expressed in the most intimate of terms – that of son to father, and moreover, as the Son of the Father. This was reflected in the way he prayed and taught others to pray and in the authority with which he spoke and acted. It is seen in his understanding of what had been revealed to him and on which his ministry was based: 'All things have been handed over to me by my Father . . . and no one knows the Father except the Son and anyone to whom the Son chooses to reveal him' (Matthew 11:27). Jesus saw himself not only as Messiah but also (uniquely) as Son of the Father.

It is perhaps right to point out that in considering these titles related to sonship, reference has frequently been made to the synoptic Gospels, while there are few such references to the Gospel of John. The nature of John's theologically rich and reflective Gospel, with its long discourses that are generally viewed as being atypical of the way Jesus taught and spoke, makes it even more difficult in a short book such as this to disentangle what might have been historical sayings of Jesus and what were later products of the post-resurrection community and John's own way of presenting his Gospel material. Biblical scholars continue to take different views on these questions, and all that has been attempted here is to outline some of the issues and the way the texts can be interpreted to help in our understanding of what the various titles could have meant to Jews of the time, to the disciples and to Jesus, and so to the early Church and to us. To see them as no more than bald statements of fact is to miss the point and their richness.

Without belittling in any way their importance, we might say that 'son of Mary', 'son of David', 'Son of Man' and 'Son of God' are titles or roles that have the force of solemn and powerful imagery conveying truths that go beyond mere factual statement. Their meaning and significance have always been subject to interpretation and, to some extent, restatement, as is most obvious with the title 'Son of God'. To see in that proof that they are mere inventions to bolster the status and reputation of a religious leader is to miss the complexity of religious experience and religious thought and to underestimate the work of the Holy Spirit in guiding the Church into an ever deeper understanding of the truth of God.

> • What are the values and the dangers in using the title 'Son of God' about Jesus?

Chapter three
The Church

a. Church as building, institution and people

There is a frequently heard complaint among certain Church leaders that when the word 'church' is used, it is wrongly assumed to mean either a building or an institution. They are anxious to correct this misunderstanding by reminding everyone that 'church' primarily means people. They are right. But before we explore that further, we should at least recognise that 'church' does also mean a building and an institution.

In rural dioceses where there are hundreds of medieval churches with minute congregations attempting to maintain them, church buildings can be a burden as well as a delight, but they are important in the mission and witness of the Christian faith. They have multiple functions: they symbolise the presence of God; they are spaces in which to worship, to learn and to socialise; they serve as a focus for communities and are assets for community activities; they contain the artefacts of centuries of devotion; they are witnesses to the glory of God although too often have been built for the glorification of patrons; they are holy spaces for consolation and for quiet reflection; the prayers of centuries have soaked into their fabric and made them holy, and they have shared in the important moments in people's lives – baptisms, weddings, funerals, celebrations and acts of remembrance. They are not to be dismissed as insignificant for faith even though they are often a drain on resources and an anxiety for Church officers, and seen by much of society as simply part of a cultural heritage of varying relevance and value.

The institutional Church, too, has its place as well as its many critics, and it exists amid the uncomfortable awareness, even among its friends, that it is far from perfect – whether it comes in Anglican, Catholic, Orthodox, Methodist, Baptist, Lutheran or whatever form. Attempts to 'be church' without taking on the trappings of organisational structures are frequently made in the effort to be truer to what the early Church is believed to have been like. Such attempts almost inevitably fail, not least because without some coordinating scaffolding the separate components fall apart or fail to survive. The early Church itself discovered this as it moved from being the gathered community of a few faithful followers in Judea into being a movement that spread throughout the Mediterranean and beyond. To prevent the fracture of endless splintering of membership, faith and practice, congregations need a way of organising themselves together. And in meeting that need, institutions are born. That they can become corrupt through the lure of power and wealth be seen in plenty of examples through history. But they also hold the possibility within themselves to be reformed and transformed through the self-regulating critique of those who hold dear the tradition of the Scriptures, the creeds and the knowledge of the example of the Church's Lord. As former Bishop of Durham David Jenkins once said, 'There are times when I cannot stand the Church, but I know also that we cannot do without it. For all its failings, and they are many, it is still necessary.'[14] It would seem that God, too, has need of the Church and, for the time being at least, ensures its continuation through the guidance of the Spirit. It is a mystery, a body both human and divine.

---

14. In a private conversation.

- In what ways do you think it is correct to say that church buildings are a burden and a delight?
- How significant do you think they are in the spreading of the gospel?

The origins of the word 'church' point very clearly to the fact that it is primarily about people, not buildings or institutions. The English word has its origins in the Germanic languages and goes back to a Byzantian word, kyrike, which meant 'belonging to the Lord'. The Church comprises those people, those congregations who acknowledge their allegiance to the Lord, who are his people.

There are similar meanings in the origin of the word 'ecclesiastic', which comes into English from Latin, originally from the Greek and related to the Hebrew. In the Greek version of the Old Testament – the Septuagint – the word ecclesia translated a Hebrew word meaning 'assembly'. 'Synagogue' also has this meaning of assembly. In itself, both in Hebrew and in Greek, the word had a secular meaning, referring to any gathering of men and women. But both in Hebrew and in Greek that basic sense was always modified in its religious usage by the notion that this was an assembly of the people of God, the people of the Lord, the assembly of Jesus Christ.

As Hans Kung pointed out in *On Being a Christian*, the word 'assembly' has the double meaning of being both the group of people gathered together and the act of gathering together.[15] He emphasised the importance of this

---

15. Hans Kung, *On Being a Christian* (Collins, 1974), pp.478ff.

second meaning which is so easily forgotten or overlooked. The Church is not a static institution of people once gathered together. It is a dynamic, organic entity that is renewed and revitalised by its coming together. The Church changes and develops, modifies and adapts even while it expresses continuity and seeks to live true to its foundations in the movement started in Palestine by a wandering preacher more than 2000 years ago. Jesus did not found a Church; he started a movement within Judaism. The Church developed as its missionary activity extended, as it moved into Gentile as well as Jewish circles, as its differences with Judaism produced a split, not least after the destruction of the temple in AD 70.

- What aspects of Christianity as a movement do you think are lost, and what are gained by the Church being an institution?

---

b. Church as body – Body of Christ

The choice to believe in Jesus Christ as Lord has to be an individual's choice. But what leads to that choice, nurtures it and helps it develop is a corporate matter. An individual's understanding of the invitation to accept the name of Christ is shaped and conveyed through the faith of the Church as a body, no matter how it presents itself. It is within that body, or even in reaction to it, that faith grows through prayer, through service, through understanding.

The Church is a body. There is in itself nothing unique about that description. Any group of people drawn together by a common purpose can be described as a body – 'a fine body of fighting men'; 'a dedicated body of caring women'. It is possible that Paul may be using the term in this way when he says, 'Gentiles have become fellow-heirs, members of the same body, and sharers in the promise of Jesus Christ through the gospel' (Ephesians 3:6). But normally there is a much deeper meaning, more mysterious and much richer in meaning. It is as the Body of Christ that the Church takes on its distinctive identity.

The description of the Church as the Body of Christ appears in the Epistles of Paul or those ascribed to Paul. In the most well-known of the passages where he uses this image he elaborates it with a telling degree of physical detail. At the beginning of 1 Corinthians 12, Paul describes the variety of gifts that the Spirit gives. He goes on to say:

> For just as the body is one and has many members, and all the members of the body, though many, are one body, so it is with Christ . . . Indeed, the body does not consist of one member but of many. If the foot were to say, 'Because I am not a hand, I do not belong to the body', that would not make it any less a part of the body . . . Now you are the body of Christ and individually members of it.

> *1 Corinthians 12:12, 14, 27*

Paul does not shy away from mentioning the 'less honourable' members of the body, and states that they are in fact given even greater honour, and the least respectable members of the body are shown greater respect, and this is how God has arranged things (1 Corinthians 12:22-4).

Paul elaborates the image to make the point that not only do members of the Church possess many and varied gifts but also they are all needed, and all have an honourable place in the life of the Church. Such gifts may express themselves in the fulfilling of certain roles appointed by God – apostles, prophets, teachers, etc. – but that doesn't mean everyone has the same gifts, nor does it mean that each of the different gifts is not valuable (1 Corinthians 12:27-30). What matters is that whatever gift or role a person has, they should also strive to have the greatest gift of all – love (1 Corinthians 12:31–13:13). And the purpose of this is 'so that the church [the Body] may be built up' (1 Corinthians 14:4, 5). Paul is encouraging those who hold particular roles in the Church not to stand on status or belittle others, as though the eye could tell the ear it is not needed, or the ear could believe itself to be the whole body. Their concern is not to be with how important they are but how well they can serve the growth and maturing of the Church, the Body.

> But speaking the truth in love, we must grow up in every way into him who is the head, into Christ, from whom the whole body, joined and knitted together by every ligament with which it is equipped, as each part is working properly, promotes the body's growth in building itself up in love.
>
> *Ephesians 4:15, 16*

He made a similar point in his letter to the Romans:

> For by the grace given to me I say to everyone among you not to think of yourself more highly than you ought to think, but to think with sober judgement, each according to the measure of faith that God has assigned. For as in

one body we have many members, and not all the members have the same function, so we, who are many, are one body in Christ, and individually we are members of one another.

Romans 12:3-5

There are a number of times when Paul emphasises the fact that he is talking about one body, the Body of Christ. The word 'one' appears repeatedly in a short passage in the letter to the Church at Ephesus: 'There is one body and one Spirit, just as you were called to the one hope of your calling, one Lord, one faith, one baptism, one God and Father of all, who is above all and through all and in all' (Ephesians 4:4-6). In Paul's time, every bit as now, there was the danger of division in the Church. There was the fear of division over questions of status, divisions over the ranking of spiritual gifts, divisions over matters such as circumcision, division over observance or not of food laws. Divisions had appeared in the congregation at Corinth. There were those who recognised Apollos as their leader; others looked to Peter; others claimed the authority of Paul as being determinative. Human beings, even Christian human beings, do not seem to find it difficult to discover reasons for disagreement and for division. 'For when one says, "I belong to Paul", and another, "I belong to Apollos", are you not merely human?' (1 Corinthians 3:4). The causes for division today may be different: divisions over churchmanship and who can be recognised as legitimately ordained; divisions over sexual orientation and gender; divisions over scriptural interpretation. The prayer of Jesus that all his followers should be one has yet to be fully realised (John 17:11).

> - How far do you think the witness of the Church is undermined by divisions within the churches and divisions between churches?

The image of the one body had implications not only for those who were already members of the Church but also for those wishing to be members. Christ is one, his Body is one, so there is only one membership. All who put their faith in Christ belong to that one Body. This meant that if Christ was the Saviour of the world, for all people and not just for Jews, then differences of race, gender or status could make no difference. All are invited, all are welcomed as members of the one Body of Christ. 'For in the one Spirit we were all baptized into one body – Jews or Greeks, slaves or free – and we were all made to drink of one Spirit' (1 Corinthians 12:13; see also Colossians 3:11). Gentiles are fellow heirs, members of the one Body (Ephesians 3:6).

In eucharistic theology there is an intertwining of meanings for the body. At one level it means the body of Christ received in the bread of Holy Communion. But this 'mystical' food is not merely the way in which the individual is spiritually sustained. The Last Supper is the sign of the heavenly banquet that the Body of all believers, the new Israel, the Church, will enjoy. So it is also that which sustains, and in many ways marks out the Church.

If members of the Church constitute the Body, then it is clear that it is Christ who is the head: 'He is the head of the body, the church; he is the beginning, the firstborn from the dead, so that he might come to have the first place in everything' (Colossians 1:18). It is God who has done this:

'He has put all things under his feet and has made him the head over all things for the church, which is his body, the fullness of him who fills all in all' (Ephesians 1:22). Paul builds up a picture of Jesus as Lord, through whom all things came into being, through whom all things adhere and through whom we have access to the Father. If, as many scholars believe, the Colossians passage comes from an earlier hymn, either Jewish or Hellenic, with the key terminology interpreted in a Christian way, 'body' may have originally referred to all of creation, the whole universe. If this is correct, the reference to the Church may have been added to bring this section in line with Paul's more common use of the body image. Even if that is the case, the idea of all creation being both brought into being through Christ and now under his rule links to the Pauline understanding of Jesus as the second Adam; the first Adam was given dominion over all creatures (Genesis 1:26), and of the Church as the first-fruits of the redeemed creation (see Romans 8:19ff).

We have seen that the use of body imagery for the Church and for Christ as its head was often elaborated to include references to other physical components such as 'members' and ligaments. Nevertheless, the simple statement that Christ is the head of the body, the Church, could be understood today as though it were saying that Christ is the chief executive (the head) of a corporation (a corporate body). It is therefore important to understand the significant distinction that appears in one of Paul's key ideas: that those who follow Christ are baptised into his name, that they are in fact 'in Christ' as well as Christ being in them. There is the sense of belonging to Christ, of having allegiance with Christ, of being 'incorporated' into Christ so that the individual's basic identity is found 'in Christ'. The idea is very important but its meaning is difficult to convey fully. Words get stretched and although Paul usually talks about being 'in Christ', he also speaks of 'putting on Christ'.

> As many of you as were baptized into Christ have clothed yourselves with Christ. There is no longer Jew or Greek, there is no longer slave or free, there is no longer male and female; for all of you are one in Christ Jesus.
>
> *Galatians 3:27, 28*

This repeats in a slightly different form the argument we saw earlier about the unity of the Body and how it overcomes all other normal distinctions of race, status and gender.

In other contexts, the notion of being 'in Christ' is contrasted with human beings being in the power of, or under the control of, sin. What Christ achieved was the defeat of sin and death so that through his death men and women who put their trust and faith in Christ were also freed from sin's power and able to obtain the promise of newness of life (see Romans 5 and 6). In his parables, Jesus used a different image – that of the vine – to convey the way in which those who follow him were to relate to him and become, as it were, part of him. He called his disciples to 'Abide in me as I abide in you. Just as the branch cannot bear fruit by itself unless it abides in the vine, neither can you unless you abide in me' (John 15:4).

Being in Christ and having Christ in them intensifies the image of the members being part of the Body. The identification of believers with Christ is intimately close. It brings with it the experience and reality of freedom from sin and reconciliation with God. It brings newness of life in the power of the Spirit of Christ who dwells within the believer. It is salvation.

For Paul, this meant that there were ethical implications for the believer as a member of the Body of Christ, and much of his time was spent dealing with quite practical ethical issues through which we discover profound theological teaching. The individual's body is a locus for the presence of God; it is the temple of the Holy Spirit and so should not be used for 'indecent' practices. But more than that, as members of Christ, believers are to be 'pure'. Most specifically they are to keep from fornication – for the fornicator sins against the body itself. 'Do you not know that your bodies are members of Christ? Should I therefore take the members of Christ and make them members of a prostitute? Never!' (1 Corinthians 6:15). Paul saw everyone who is in Christ as being a 'new creation', and as such they should behave accordingly (2 Corinthians 5:17). As members of Christ and in Christ believers receive his peace and his love. It was incumbent upon them, and it is incumbent upon us, to live in peace and in love in the way of Christ, doing everything in the name of the Lord Jesus (Colossians 3:12-17).

- What impact do you think being 'in Christ' should have on a Christian?
- Is it a phrase you find helpful in describing your relationship with Christ?

Epilogue

The mystery of God eludes all our doctrinal definitions, our descriptions in story or hymnody, our depictions in music, art or sculpture. It is inevitable that it is so. It is also inevitable that we continue to make the effort to give shape to those glimpses and intimations of God that we have. Many people find it helpful to have some kind of picture of God in their mind when they pray, be that of the Father or of Jesus.

That our relationship with God and our understanding of who God is should draw upon images associated with our own physical bodies and experience is unsurprising since Christians affirm the personal nature of the God they worship. Such suggestions as 'Ground of Being' as a description of God may have their insights, but they can also feel rather abstract. For many, they lack the personal warmth and intimacy conveyed by words such as 'Father'.

For all their aversion to images of God, even the Jews found themselves attributing to God physical features as they sought to convey what he meant to them and how he related to them. Without ever describing it in detail, they looked for God's face turned towards them and felt distraught when he hid his face from them. They wrote of God's eyes looking upon them with mercy and sometimes in anger. They believed he spoke to them and that prophets heard his voice and conveyed the messages they had received. In times of distress the people sought the support and sustaining comfort of God's arms and saw his activity in the works of his hands. In doing so the people and the prophets and the psalmists were using the language of poetic imagery, not the language of anatomy. At their best they were well aware of the danger of making God in their own image rather than seeing themselves as made in God's image.

Most radical of all is the belief that in Jesus God did in fact appear in physical form as a human being – the Word made flesh. He became man and lived among us, a particular man in a particular place at a particular time. For all the efforts of painters and sculptors, we still do not really know what Jesus looked like in any detail. And perhaps it is just as well. It makes it easier for us to understand that in him all people, all races, all conditions of men and women are drawn together and find their salvation.

The Gospel writers often draw upon aspects of Jesus' physical form to help convey their theological understanding of what his words and actions meant. In all this it is meaning that is important, conveyed by imagery that is nuanced and intricate in its richness and delicacy, rooted in the very physicality of a body. It gives value and worth to our own bodies although we believe that, as with the mystery of God, there is also mystery in being human – a mystery that our bodies speak of, but they do not tell everything.